BRIDGING
CULTURES

BRIDGING
CULTURES
ETHNIC
SERVICES
IN THE LIBRARIES
OF NEW YORK STATE

EDITED BY

Irina A. Kuharets
Brigid A. Cahalan
Fred J. Gitner

WITH A FOREWORD BY

Susan Lehman Keitel

NEW YORK LIBRARY ASSOCIATION
ETHNIC SERVICES ROUND TABLE
ALBANY · NEW YORK · 2001

New York Library Association/Ethnic Services Round Table
Albany, New York
©2001 by NYLA/ESRT
All rights reserved. Published 2001
Cover drawing by Igor Kopelnitsky
Electronic imaging and book design by Irina A. Kuharets
Printed in the United States of America
ISBN 0-931658-48-9
New York Library Association
252 Hudson Avenue
Albany, NY 12210-1802
www.nyla.org

To

DAVID COHEN

Advocate, mentor and friend

ETHNIC
SERVICES
IN THE LIBRARIES
OF NEW YORK STATE

CONTENTS

(Under each city articles are arranged alphabetically by title)

FOREWORD

The Ethnic Services Round Table of the New York Library Association has been unwavering in its mission to see that the libraries of New York State offer multicultural services and programs to their diverse patrons. The Round Table's diligence and outreach efforts have made it possible for librarians and trustees throughout this state to avail themselves of information about a rich array of multicultural programs that have been proven successful. With the history, hints and help that the Round Table offers, no librarian need feel alone in trying to identify and serve patrons from geographies as various as Bangladesh, China, Haiti, Korea, Poland, Russia, and the many Spanish-speaking countries of Latin America, to mention a few. NYLA is indeed grateful for the commitment and careful work of the members of the Round Table and is proud to have been able to support and encourage their efforts in publishing this collection of essays.

— SUSAN LEHMAN KEITEL
Executive Director, New York Library Association

PREFACE

How does one determine the worth of a library? Today—perhaps
more than at any time in the past—a good measure of a library's
worth is its dedication to serving ethnic populations. Fast-growing
ethnic communities throughout New York State and the entire
country call for librarians who are knowledgeable, conscientious
and enthusiastic about multicultural services. Over the last few
decades, many libraries have re-examined policies and expanded
and strengthened them to better serve diverse communities.

The personal efforts of colleagues who have shown leadership
in this area need to be shared and one opportunity to do so arose
at the 1999 NYLA Annual Conference in Buffalo. At the conference, the Ethnic Services Round Table of the New York Library
Association held its first Multicultural Expo. Participating librarians shared with Expo attendees their experiences in serving ethnic
populations in the libraries throughout New York State—academic
and public, large and small, urban, rural and suburban. Noting
that multiculturalism is not limited to communities traditionally
seen as cosmopolitan, Homa Naficy (1998–99 ESRT President who
launched the Expo) commented that: "We are exposed to world
cultures in the music we hear, the books we read, the food we eat,
and the fashions we wear. Libraries offering multicultural services
are responding to today's spirit of multiculturalism" ("Multiculturalism: The Spirit of New York Libraries," in *NYSALB Trustee*,
Vol.XI, No.3, July 2000). The success stories recounted during
Expo'99 conveyed valuable information for all librarians serving

multicultural communities in New York State. Unfortunately, many of our colleagues who are very interested in this topic could not attend Expo '99. In order to facilitate an exchange of ideas among a wider group, the ESRT Executive Board decided to publish a book of articles written by librarians about their first-hand experiences in serving ethnic populations. Articles were solicited through announcements placed in the *NYLA Bulletin* and the NY-LINE Listserv during the year 2000. Many librarians from all over the state expressed a willingness to participate, setting the stage for this publication. While the Expo '99 program allowed for an immediate exchange of experiences and ideas through personal interactions, the book offers its own rewards: a greater number of librarians sharing their experiences and a wider audience learning from those experiences.

The intent of this volume is not to cover the full range of ethnic services offered by librarians throughout New York State. Instead, each author was given free range to describe his/her personal experiences and was left with the responsibility of ensuring the accuracy of names, dates and facts described in his/her work. Efforts were made to preserve the original style of writing. The editing was done very largely by Brigid Cahalan and Fred Gitner. Their professional knowledge, dedication to every aspect of the book, enthusiasm, and willingness to put in many hours of personal time, made this volume possible.

This book is a showcase of exemplary services to African Americans, Native Americans, and Spanish speakers, as well as to communities of Chinese, Cambodians, Russians and others in our state. Written in various styles, ranging from warmly personal to formal, the essays describe library programs and services for children, young adults and adults, as well as achievements in information technology and outreach services. The articles, some of which give fascinating historical perspectives, will inspire and guide library staff in serving ethnic populations.

The book opens with an article by Professor David Cohen, excerpted from his essay published in the eighties on the issue of

xiv

multiculturalism in the United States. Mr. Cohen, a former adjunct professor in the Graduate School of Library and Information Studies of Queens College of the City University of New York, is a distinguished contributor to research in multicultural librarianship, particularly on the role of librarians and the availability of multicultural material. Two of his pieces are included to give readers an historical background for multicultural issues and ethnic services.

We are particularly indebted to Professor Cohen, who was the founder and driving force of ESRT for two decades. During that time he has also been a mentor for librarians concerned with issues of improving ethnic services to the underserved in libraries. Today, he continues to inspire us to meet new challenges. With admiration and gratitude for his major contribution in advancing numerous issues in the cause of multicultural librarianship, the authors dedicate this volume to Professor David Cohen.

We are also deeply grateful to Russian House, Inc. for its monetary support, which covered part of the printing costs. A special thanks goes to artist Igor Kopelnitsky for his drawing for the front cover. On behalf of the ESRT Editorial Committee and all of the contributing authors, thank you to those—too many to mention by name—who have assisted us in various ways to make this publication possible.

Irina A. Kuharets
Chair, ESRT Editorial Committee

ADVANCES IN ETHNICITY AND LIBRARIANSHIP
IN NEW YORK STATE AND AROUND THE COUNTRY

By David Cohen

Part I. Ethnicity in Librarianship

(The following article is excerpted from an essay by David Cohen entitled "Ethnicity in Librarianship: A Rationale for Multiethnic Library Services in a Heterogeneous Society," which appeared in the Fall 1980 issue of *Library Trends*.)

In the United States the notion that ethnicity is "in" is certainly encouraged by the multiplicity of references to it in both scholarly and popular sources of information. The struggle for recognition by racial and ethnic minorities, instigated by the Black power movement in the 1960s, has catapulted into sharp focus the concept that America, far from being a "melting pot," is a country best described by such words as pluralistic, multicultural and multiethnic. "Ethnic pluralism" refers to the variety of ethnic minorities, each of which wants equality of opportunity in addition to a group identity that will be accepted by all other groups in society. It is typical of ethnic minorities that they do not have sufficient power to fulfill their needs and are constantly striving to overcome discrimination, prejudice and stereotyping.

In its simplest definition, the condition of belonging to a particular ethnic group constitutes "ethnicity." A concomitant quality is ethnic pride. As a new concept, ethnicity has been in a state of constant growth and development since Glazer and Moynihan startled us with their book *Beyond the Melting Pot*, which underscored the existence of ethnic enclaves in the neighborhoods of New York. Instead of homogenized, assimilated Americans, they found heterogeneous national groups identified particularly by their cultural differences and special interests.

In essence, ethnicity rejects assimilation as well as separatism and thrives on a positive, irreducible diversity. It is especially suited for the defense of minority rights, which may be impaired, however, by manifestations of chauvinism and racism.

To understand ethnicity one must know a good deal about the physical, linguistic, cultural, and religious characteristics typical of an ethnic group. People in a society who share a historic identity and consciousness based on cultural commonality or territorial ties, or a group of the same race or national origin, speaking the same language and/or sharing a common, distinctive culture, constitute such a group. Common racial identity alone does not make an ethnic group; a sharing of history and cultural tradition is necessary.

Librarianship is closely related to ethnicity in that it intends to serve all the people in the community and so must find ways to reach people from all the ethnic groups in the library orbit, users and nonusers. This relationship can only be maintained on a continuing fruitful basis by means of creative collection building and innovative programs and services for these ethnic groups. In order to do this successfully as professionals, we must have a thorough understanding of and sensitivity to the factor of ethnicity in the heritage, behavior and lifestyles of the people in the local community.

Development of Programs and Services with an Ethnic Content

In order to design library programs with an ethnic content, there must be a gestalt, an integrated approach based on the understanding that we live in a country not only pluralistic in the general sense, but multiethnic. For the past fifteen years, under pressure from ethnic and professional groups, publishers have made significant strides in making available library materials dealing with ethnic minorities. Library collections already reflect this significant output by the publishing world. This does not mean we have solved the problem of providing sufficient and adequate multiethnic materials. Clearly, we can still use more and better-quality materials that deal with ethnicity. However, it is important that the ethnic patrons for whom these materials are intended be drawn into the library orbit by alert and understanding professionals who are prepared with services meaningful to these patrons. The dividend for the profession in successful approaches to the ethnic minorities is that these citizens become not only friends of the library, but also stalwart and vigorous supporters of libraries around budget time.

Following is a concise outline of a document prepared for the 1979 White House Conference on Library and Information Services entitled, *Issues and Resolutions: A Summary of Pre-Conference Activities.*

Libraries should:

1. Place a high priority on determining the ethnic makeup of the community to develop relevant collections and services.
2. Extend ethnic services.
3. Set up programs designed to acquaint librarians with multicultural literature.
4. Recruit volunteers of all ethnic backgrounds and provide orientation, coordination and continuing education.
5. Develop collections that reflect the cultural heritage of the community.
6. Maintain up-to-date collections with materials reflecting the minority characteristics of the American society.
7. Designate one library as a multi-ethnic branch where cultural and ethnic materials are housed and personnel are trained and knowledgeable.

8. Through public service announcements, emphasize to the public the need and importance of preserving our past records and history.
9. Present television documentaries of past events and their effect on the lifestyle we have grown accustomed to.

As public libraries develop programs and services for ethnic groups they should keep in mind the following basic principles:

1. There must be a strong community involvement in the design and operation of all programs, once it has been ascertained that they are needed and desirable.
2. Finely tuned service delivery systems, which take into account cultural patterns and traditions, must be built on the existing community network of neighborhoods, church, ethnic, and social groups.
3. Trained professionals must be thoroughly sensitized to the social, familial, ethnic, economic, and political characteristics of the people in their neighborhoods.

Educational institutions should:

1. Include required courses on ethnic, cultural, bilingual and human relations in the education curriculum for librarianship.
2. Provide schools with library collections, which include literature depicting varied cultures and ethnic groups in a realistic manner.

This is a creative and demanding grassroots agenda, which should be followed up with tremendous lobbying efforts by professionals and citizens who believe a multiethnic America needs to be strengthened and unified by library services with a multiethnic content.

In conclusion, the library profession can advance human intergroup relations by its concerns, commitment and extraordinary services to the ethnic groups in the urban centers of the United States.

Part II. Beyond the Melting Pot

(The following is excerpted from an article by David Cohen and Suzanne Li entitled "Beyond the Melting Pot: School Library Media Center Resources for Dealing with the World of Difference" which appeared in *The Bookmark*, Volume 50, Number 1, Fall 1991.)

On May 14, 1990, a panel of distinguished discussants at The New York Public Library celebrated the 20th anniversary of the second edition of Daniel P. Moynihan's seminal work, *Beyond the Melting Pot*. The underlying theme of *Beyond the Melting Pot* seems more evident today than when the first edition was published in 1963; where race is concerned, the melting pot metaphor doesn't stand up.

At the May 1990 meeting, Moynihan and Glazer pointed out that their goal was not so much to celebrate ethnicity, but to come to grips with the divisions of society. They said that they had not anticipated the subsequent surge in immigration to New York from the Caribbean, Latin America, Korea, China, Vietnam and the Soviet Union. They further noted the general failure of American-born Blacks to be swept into the city's economic and social mainstream and, with Puerto Ricans, their status as part of a great dependent class.

An article on the demography of our population, also entitled "Beyond the Melting Pot," appeared in *Time* magazine (4/9/90, pp. 28–31). The question the author raises is what will the U.S. be like when whites are no longer the majority? The alternative title is

"America's Changing Colors" — and the substance of the message is that in the twenty-first century, now just around the corner, racial and ethnic groups will outnumber whites for the first time. The "browning" of America will alter everything in society from politics and education to industry, values, and culture and, necessarily, library services.

What is the Impact on Schools and Libraries?

In California, the State Librarian took the initiative, calling a statewide conference in the summer of 1988 to focus anew on library services to the ethnic and racial minorities in California, which will approach the 50 percent mark by the year 2000. The conference included professionals, politicians and community people who made important recommendations in all aspects of librarianship to cope with the "new majority" in the population. The technique of using open forums for community participation produced some very creative results. These recommendations were reported in the conference proceedings, *A State of Change: California's Ethnic Future and Libraries* (1988). We need to examine those ideas, e.g., on recruitment and education of librarians to support a multicultural thrust in librarianship in New York State.

At Queens College Graduate School of Library and Information Studies we now offer a course on "Multicultural Librarianship: Materials and Services." This title represents a significant change in point of view. The previous title, which had been in the curriculum for the last fifteen years, was "Minority Materials and Services in Libraries." Over the years, to support this course, we developed a special and distinct multiethnic collection of materials, now housed in the Rosenthal Library of Queens College as a separate entity.

Recent Developments

The New York Governor's Conference on Library and Information Services in Albany, November 28-30, 1990, approved two pertinent resolutions:

Diversity: "The Governor's Conference supports cultural diversity in all its forms. Accordingly, libraries should encourage diversity among its patrons, its staff, and its collections and services . . ."(CR 1087)

Multicultural Librarianship: "Library Services should develop regular programs and build collections for New York's populations to reflect a multicultural theme relevant in all communities . . ."(CR 4001)

On the national front, the White House Conference on Library and Information Services in Washington, D.C., July 9-13, 1991, approved the following recommendations relevant to multiculturalism and the role of school library media centers: multicultural and multilingual services: "The President and Congress shall pass legislation to authorize and fund a program which provides (a) financial and technical assistance for library and information services for multicultural and multilingual populations, (b) a national database of multicultural, multilingual materials for use by libraries and information services, including research and demonstration projects on model library programs serving our multicultural and multilingual populations. . ."

A petition recommendation says that "The United States Department of Education shall acknowledge the number of children from multicultural, multilingual populations who are being served by the nation's schools by emphasizing the establishment and strengthening of school library media programs in every school in the nation; by encouraging the development of curricula which values and celebrates the nation's pluralism and diversity . . ." (Petition 08, part 6)

These events at the state and national levels put our schools and libraries on notice: we must face the challenge of providing the multicultural resources needed for learning and understanding. Multicultural education can only be as effective as the materials teachers use to develop learning experiences for children and youth. The dangers of using materials that perpetuate bias, racism, stereotyping and inaccurate information on ethnic, racial and cultural groups are obvious.

To deal with the truth about diversity in our history will not be easy. Doubts about multicultural perspectives must be resolved, even as we become more diverse. By the year 2000, one out of every three New Yorkers will come from a minority group and librarians can help understand and interpret the "world of difference" by providing solid materials on ethnicity and multiculturalism for our public.

1999 NYLA ANNUAL CONFERENCE
BUFFALO, N.Y.

Ethnic Services Round Table Presents
NYLA'S FIRST
Multicultural Expo '99

Buffalo Convention Center Exhibit Hall
During No-Conflict Exhibit Hours

ALL NYLA CONFERENCE ATTENDEES ARE INVITED

Day One! Thursday, October 28, 5:00 to 6:00 p.m.
GAMES FROM MANY LANDS

Explore the fascinating origins and significance of games from many lands. Try your hand at Yote, Backgammon, Tangram, Parcheesi, Mancala ... and get a chance to win a prize!

Day Two! Friday, October 29, 1:30 to 3:00 p.m.
LIBRARY SUCCESS STORIES

Interact face-to-face with library representatives as they share examples of successful community partnerships, programs, publicity, staff recruitment, and electronic information resources designed to serve New York's diverse ethnic communities and promote cross-cultural understanding. (Presentations will be made using a poster session/table talk format.)

Funding for this program was generously provided by the Reader's Digest Foundation

NYLA/ESRT Multicultural Expo '99 flyer. Designed by Homa Naficy

JUST PLAY IT!
GAMES FROM MANY LANDS

By Zahra M. Baird and Jennifer L. Ransom

"Want to play a game?" Ask this question to anyone, and chances are that they will say, "Yes!" No matter what age we are, games appeal to us. Games can help us learn skills, develop strategies, and are a lot of fun. Games originate in a wide variety of countries. Some games, due to travel, have been adapted from place to place. Long ago, games were played in cultures where strong community spirit and the need for group cooperation were necessary for survival. Games can also help to bridge cultures and foster an understanding of world cultures.

The Ethnic Services Round Table members at the conference planning meeting decided to bring together people to play games from all over the world. We planned "Games From Many Lands," as part of ESRT's Multicultural Expo, for the 1999 NYLA Conference in Buffalo, New York. The session took place during a no-conflict time on Thursday, October 28, 1999 from 5:00 to 6:00 P.M.—that was the first day of the Expo, which was scheduled for two days. "Games" targeted a diverse audience of NYLA conference attendees including librarians, educators, library staff, and trustees. We set out with three goals: introducing world cultures in a fun manner; providing information for attendees to take back, share with colleagues, and use in their own libraries and communities; and highlighting the value of games in modern society.

The first step was research. We found several books with information about games from many lands and their origins. (A bibliography is included at the end of this article.) One of the books we found most helpful was *The Multicultural Game Book: More than 70 Traditional Games from 30 Countries* by Louise Orlando. It provides information on games from a wide variety of cultures explained in easy-to-understand language. Orlando presents each game in a clear, organized format—Place of Origin, Skills, Ages, Players, Materials, Background Information, and Rules of Play. We found that many games from different countries are similar but have different names. Variations of games have sprouted up throughout the centuries.

The key players who contributed to this program were: Homa Naficy, 1999 President of ESRT, who wrote a grant to obtain funds for the Multicultural Expo; Zahra Baird and Jennifer Ransom, who co-chaired the Games Committee; Rosemary Mesh, Irina Kuharets, and Tom Brogan, who were committee members; and the twenty-five ESRT members who volunteered to staff the game tables, where they provided instruction and played the games with attendees.

Preparation took approximately two weeks of solid planning spread over three months on a part-time basis. During that time, we played the games with friends, co-workers, and family members. This was fun! We began by compiling a list of twenty-five games we considered the most enjoyable. We developed the following criteria to be met for inclusion—Is the game easy to set up? Does it use minimal equipment? Is it easy to play keeping in mind space and time constraints? Is there enough variety in the countries of origin and type of game (strategy, board game, etc.)? Some games were eliminated for various reasons: Cribbage (European) and Mah Jongg (China) due to the complexity of rules; Piñata (Mexico) due to safety hazards; and Hopscotch (Aruba, Bolivia, Czechoslovakia, Germany, Poland, Trinidad, etc.) due to space constraints.

We were left with twelve games: Backgammon (Persia, India, Rome), Dominoes (China), Yo-Yo (Ancient China and Rome), Pachisi (India), String Games (Native North Americans), Solitaire (France), Mancala (Africa and Asia), Nimbi (Denmark), Tangrams

(Ancient China), Checkers (Europe), Chinese Checkers, and Yote (Ancient African game of checkers).

Most of the games were purchased for $10 each at neighborhood stores, such as K-B Toys, Toys-R-Us, The Educational Warehouse, and The Museum Company Store. We made materials for Tangrams (out of cardboard) and String Games (string cords), which we handed out to the participants along with detailed examples of activities they could share with others. Two hundred yo-yos were donated by the Scarsdale Public Library, a member of the Westchester Library System, to distribute to participants. We laminated game instructions for perusal at each table and had copies of game instructions for participants to take home with them. The volunteers who staffed the game tables were provided with instructions for their games well before the conference to allow them ample time to become comfortable playing the game and demonstrating it to others.

One hundred attendees participated in the program by playing at least one game. Participants gave us verbal feedback on the spot. In this way, we discovered that they enjoyed playing games they previously had no interest in or thought too difficult. Some of the participants requested that we mail them additional information to be used in their libraries or classrooms. Another hundred conference attendees walked through the area to observe the activities and to learn more about the games. It was heartwarming to see how many people came out in friendly competition and came away knowing much more about other cultures' ways of playing together.

The two-day Multicultural Expo was funded by the Readers' Digest Foundation. Homa Naficy, 1999 president of ESRT, wrote the proposal for the grant awarded in the amount of $2,500. Funds were used to cover the cost of renting tables in the Conference Exhibit Hall, and the cost of promotional items, such as publicity flyers, buttons, magnets—all included in packets distributed to the participants, together with informational handouts. Approximately $100 was spent on the purchase of the games and

Rosalind Matzner (*left*) and Charlotte Clark of Queens Borough Public Library
enjoy a game of Solitaire. Photo by Zahra M. Baird

$100 was spent on a wooden boxed set of various games, which was raffled off at the end of the Games Program.

The Multicultural Expo was publicized in the NYLA Conference Bulletin, and the NYLA Conference Program. Flyers were included in the registration packets of conference attendees. On the first day of the Expo, before the games began, members of a local Chinese organization paraded throughout the Exhibit Hall in a traditional Chinese Dragon costume, attracting attendees to the opening of the Expo and to its first program — "Games From Many Lands." Announcements were made in the Exhibit Hall inviting attendees to participate in the Multicultural Expo.

Dozens of participants enthusiastically approached us with positive feedback about their "Games" experience. Since, however, there is always room for improvement, in retrospect we would have done better to have more visuals, such as maps, flags, coats-of-arms, and, if possible, traditional dress from the countries of origin of the games. Although some of the volunteers staffed a table at which a game from their native country was played, we would have liked to have more of these ethnic pairings. Displaying fact books, and folktales and legends from each game's country of origin would have extended the cultural learning experience. Having the participants complete an evaluation form to elicit feedback would have ensured the collection of statistical and empirical data.

Playing games is a universal activity that unifies people and offers them an opportunity to interact with each other. Although our focus was bringing together conference attendees, "Games from Many Lands" would be an appropriate program to present to an intergenerational public in many settings including academic, public and school libraries. This idea could also be used to bring staff together or to partner with community agencies in presenting multicultural programming, such as celebrating heritage days. In fact, after participating in the "Games from Many Lands" program, some participants expressed their enthusiasm for holding a multicultural games program of their own. Playing together is not only fun but can also be valuable for team building and learning about cultures.

Let the games begin!

Resources bookmark for "Games from Many Lands" designed by Homa Naficy and distributed to attendees at NYLA/ESRT Multicultural Expo '99

Appendix

Resources for "Games from Many Lands" program

Board Games 'Round the World: A Resource Book for Mathematical Investigation by Robbie Bell and Michael Cornelius (Cambridge Press University, 1989).

Cat's Cradle, Owl's Eyes: A Book of String Games by Camilla Gryski (William Morrow and Company, 1984).

Children's Traditional Games: Games from 137 Countries and Cultures by Robert Kaminski and Judy Sierra (Oryx Press, 1995).

Dominoes Around the World by Mary Lankford (Morrow Junior Books, 1998).

Games From Long Ago by Bobbie Kalman and David Schimpky (Crabtree Publishing Company, 1995).

Great Games Book: Over 30 Popular Games to Make and Play From Around the World by Susan Adams (DK, 1997).

Hands Around the World: 365 Creative Ways to Build Cultural Awareness and Global Respect by Susan Milord (Williamson Publishing Company, 1992).

Hopscotch Around the World by Mary Lankford (William Morrow and Company, 1992).

Jacks Around the World by Mary Lankford (William Morrow and Company, 1996).

Juba This and Juba That: 100 African American Games for Children by Darlene Powell Hopson and Derek S. Hopson (Simon and Schuster, 1996).

Let's Play: Traditional Games of Childhood by Camilla Gryski (Kids Can Press, 1998).

Multicultural Game Book: More Than 70 Traditional Games from 30 Countries by Louise Orlando (Scholastic Professional Books, 1993). *Sidewalk Games Around the World* by Arlene Erlbach (Millbrook Press, 1997).

You Can Yo-Yo! 25 Tricks to Try by Bruce Weber (Scholastic Inc., 1998).

Compiled by Timothy A. Baird, Adult Services Librarian at White Plains Public Library and Zahra M. Baird

AMHERST

AMHERST PUBLIC LIBRARY
OUR PATH TO SERVICE FOR ETHNIC GROUPS
IN THE COMMUNITY

By Mary F. Bobinski

We all have our dreams. For many years, I had a dream of better service to our community with regard to multicultural materials and programs. But with a limited budget and an already over-worked staff in the busiest libraries in Erie County, time went by, and the only inroad I was able to achieve was to include some multicultural programs on my twice-weekly half-hour show on cable TV.

Then ten years ago, in 1991, the first of our fortuitous events occurred. A new library school graduate named Gwen Kistner appeared at our doorstep. Enthusiastic, outgoing and service-minded, she was eager to get started in the profession and would take any hours of employment we might have. We didn't have any full-time work available, but as I talked to her the need to serve our multicultural groups seemed to match her potential abilities. I thought that I now might have the opportunity to get going on a project very dear to my heart. At first I guided her into what I thought was needed—a series of programs directed to the most recently-arrived ethnic groups in the Amherst community. In checking the data in our three local school districts at the time, I learned that the three largest new immigrant groups were Chinese, Korean and Indian. I thought that some really festive evening family programs showcasing all aspects of the culture—literature, music, art, dance and food—would be fun for the ethnic group involved, bring them into the library, and also help our community appreciate other cultures.

At first I helped Gwen, providing her with names of people I had used as guests on my TV shows and contacts at some major community organizations, who might be helpful. Then, Gwen took off. Her results, with the auditorium filled to capacity at fun-filled programs, netted me the fulfillment of part of my dream—we were finally beginning to reach an underserved part of the community. Gwen's success in this endeavor led to the creation of a full-time position within a brief period of time.

Each multicultural program was accompanied by displays of books and artifacts in the library showcases and special collections of books and materials for checkout. The initial program on China featured a lion dance by the University at Buffalo Red Lion Dancers, a food demonstration by Steven Fu, owner of Emperor's Wok, and a calligraphy demonstration by Dr. Yow-Wu, a professor at the University at Buffalo. This was followed by a Korean program with a painting demonstration by artist Nan-Pa Yoo, a demonstration of Tae Kwon Do, a parade of costumes, and food tasting. Next was a program on India with a dance presentation by Tejaswini Yayathi and Disciples, food with Raj Chhiber, owner of Raj Mahal Restaurant, classical music of India by Arvind Goel and friends, as well as Indian crafts by Gurukul.

These first few programs led to involvement in specialized programs by more than a dozen ethnic groups including Greek, Russian, Mexican, Polish, African American, Irish, Scottish, Japanese, Hawaiian and Ukrainian, among others. The results provided by these cultural connections are beyond description. Bringing all these people into the libraries, letting them know that we cared about them, highlighting the offerings of materials to help serve them, and celebrating their contributions to our community, were heart-warming experiences for our staff.

Our cultural evenings were party nights. People clapped, laughed, danced, sang and enjoyed themselves so much that they didn't want to leave. Everyone learned a lot, not only about the

culture and food, but also about the customs and games. We all
had fun getting to know each other. And we hoped that these

Flyer for Korean Cultural Night held in October 1992 at Amherst Public Library
as part of the "Fall Festival of Cultural Visions"

friendships would continue as ethnic groups felt welcomed and became acclimatized to our community.

Suhasimi Sumithra performing an Indian dance as part of East Indian Cultural Night held in August 1997 at Amherst Public Library. Photo by Gwen Kistner

Gwen Kistner does a fantastic job with these programs and her contacts with the ethnic groups and organizations in our community have grown from my initial groups to countless others including universities, schools, student associations, clubs, churches, restaurants and stores.

Then, to add frosting to the cake, about four years ago we had an opportunity to select a new branch manager in Amherst. Who should I find on the list but Judith Lopez del Moral, who was serving as Coordinator of the Life-Long Learning Center at the Central Library in Buffalo, with special responsibilities for outreach to immigrant populations! She had taught English in Poland

and Russia and participated in an educational exchange in Lille, France. Judi was happy to join us, and I was delighted to have another staff member whose interest and background in literacy and in serving ethnic groups were strong. Judi currently serves on the boards of Literacy Volunteers in Buffalo, New York, and NYLA's Ethnic Services Round Table. Two years ago, she was awarded a grant from the New York State Department of Library Development for Adult Literacy Services. With this grant we established a collection of books, media, hardware and software for the four Amherst libraries. Along with this, Judi, in conjunction with Literacy Volunteers, started group English conversation classes, which still continue. The conversations focus on world cultures, shared similarities and introduction to everyday life in America. Other programs were offered along with these classes, including a Polish butter lamb demonstration workshop, a Mardi Gras party, and the celebration of the Chinese New Year during the Year of the Dragon. Judi also conducted a series of programs entitled, "What on Earth Is Going On." These included aspects of Buddhist Tibet, the Amazon Rain Forest, the Rwandan Civil War and the economic implications of the Chinese takeover of Hong Kong.

However, I have never felt that we had completely filled the library needs of the ethnic members of our community. The numbers and variety of ethnic groups in our communities continue to grow. In the past few years, there has been an influx of Russians in Amherst. Again, serendipitously, Lana Okhotina Shmelkina, an applicant for a page position, appeared at our door. There was some concern on the part of our staff as to what contribution she might make. She was having difficulty with the Library of Congress Classification System used in our library because of the differences between the Cyrillic and Roman alphabets. However, we kept her on, trained her in various tasks, and she soon became a valued member of the staff. When I became aware of the increase in our Russian population, I was delighted to be able to set up a Russian collection with Lana's help. We now have newspapers, magazines and books in Russian, which the Russian community loves.

All of our programs are free to the public and are usually publicized in English, with a few phrases in other languages. Posters are printed and publicity sent to all news, radio and TV media. We post flyers to advertise programs in schools, community centers and housing projects as well.

In addition to programs and collections, we have an Activity Center at the Amherst Main Library at Audubon, with educational toys, games, books and materials for very young children, which has been much appreciated by ethnic families in our community.

I am pleased that each day we are better able to give needed service to the various ethnic groups in the community. It seems that with dreams and vision, opportunity and dedicated staff members, lack of money and resources should not stand in the way of what we would like to do. Of course, we would be pleased to have more money and staff for this purpose, especially to put our publicity into languages other than English. But, we are proud of what we have been able to accomplish with no great increases in budget, limited resources and limited staff. We can do it, and if we want to provide better service to our community, we must!

AMSTERDAM

ETHNIC HARMONY

By Esther Dean and Sally Romano

Located in the beautiful Mohawk Valley, the Amsterdam Free Library is at the center of Amsterdam's downtown. The library is truly the heart of our community. It was originally established in the 1800's as a library society and in 1891 became a subscription library known as the Amsterdam Library Association. In 1902, it officially became known as the Amsterdam Free Library, when Andrew Carnegie donated funds toward the building of the existing historic landmark, which was completed in 1903. The original structure stands to this day as an authentic Carnegie Library.

In 1998 and 1999 Amsterdam Free Library very successfully presented two multicultural series funded by a New York State Council on the Arts Decentralization Grant and the Friends of the Amsterdam Free Library. Both programs were geared toward a family audience, ranging in age from children to senior citizens, with the goal of introducing our community to the different ways people from all cultures express themselves through their music, dance, storytelling and arts and crafts traditions.

Planning the programs was accomplished over a two-year period by four Children's Department staff members, who compiled information on each cultural group represented, and contacted potential performers and community groups. Contacts were made with the Knights of Lithuania, The American Polonaise Society, the Irish American Club, Centro Cívico Hispano-American Organization, St. Agnello Club, the Mohawk Indian Community at

Kanatsiohareke Capital District and the Mohawk Valley Wood-carvers Association.

The planning/preparation of the projects took approximately ten hours a month for the duration of each series (six months). The writing of the grant application took an estimated six hours and producing and distributing publicity and press releases, an estimated three hours per event. Staff time used to host each event consisted of one hour prior to and one hour following the event.

Publicity for each event was distributed to about thirty local businesses, schools, three local radio stations, public access television, four local newspapers, member libraries, the library's Friends newsletter, community event calendars, and our own library.

All events were held at the Amsterdam Free Library in the second floor Children's Department. The library, which is centrally located in the city of Amsterdam, is served by public transportation. The building is accessible to the handicapped, although the second floor does not have wheelchair access. All programs were offered free of charge and were open to the public. Attendees ranged in age from pre-school children to senior citizens. Some programs were scarcely attended while others were overwhelmingly attended. Attendance depended widely on factors of weather, date and time of event, conflicting community and school events and general interest of the community. Each event was publicized in English using flyers and posters. Press releases were distributed a minimum of two weeks prior to the event.

The Earth Harmonies series explored ways in which people from a variety of cultures expressed themselves through their music and art. Programs were presented as a dual series of four musical concerts and four Saturday morning cultural demonstrations/craft workshops attended by 478 community members.

The Melting Pot series concentrated on the heritage of the people in the Mohawk Valley and Adirondack region through performances of music, dance and storytelling. The second component of the series included demonstrations/craft programs focusing on the Early American, Chinese American, Irish American and

Native American traditions. The five performance programs entertained 179 children and adults and the second component attracted 222 to the Saturday morning events. Local newspapers covered most of the presentations prior to and during the events.

Amsterdam Free Library

presents a family event

Lithuanian Heritage Program

with the

Knights of Lithuania

Saturday, April 18th
at 10:30 a.m.

Traditions • Crafts • Dance

Free and open to all • Please call 842-1080 for reservations

This program is made possible, in part, with funds from the New York State Council on the Arts Decentralization Program administered in Fulton, Montgomery and Schoharie Counties by the Schoharie County Arts Council, Inc.

Flyer for Lithuanian Heritage Program presented at Amsterdam Free Library in 1998 as part of the series entitled, "Earth Harmonies: Music and Arts Around the World"

The library has been pleased with the overall positive response to the events held. We hope to bridge the gap between the many ethnic groups in the surrounding communities by continuing to provide family programs in a non-threatening atmosphere. Our next exciting project, funded by the Schoharie County Arts Council's NYSCA Decentralization Grant, was a series entitled: "Traditions: Yesterday, Today and Tomorrow," which was held in the spring of 2001. Through performances and workshops, we experienced multicultural arts as handed down from generation to generation. Performances of traditional Chinese dance, Japanese paper craft, Native American legends, puppetry and ventriloquism were presented to show the many ways ethnic cultures have survived the passage of time.

The opportunity to present programs of a multicultural nature has been a rewarding and positive experience for staff and members of the library community. We are optimistic that our future ethnic programming endeavors will continue to thrive through available grant support and enthusiastic audience participation.

BUFFALO

AFRICAN AMERICAN WRITERS' RECEPTION

By Suzanne Jacobs

For the past six years, as part of National Library Week, the African American Writers' Reception has been held at the Buffalo & Erie County Public Library System's Martin Luther King Branch. The King Library is a small branch located in a residential, African American neighborhood. It is an atypical library in that it is situated in leased space in a shopping plaza. Much of the neighborhood is comprised of public housing projects with a recent influx of new single family homes. The 2000 Population and Housing census describes the neighborhood as a high poverty area near downtown Buffalo. The celebration continues to pay tribute to local African American writers of Western New York. This popular event provides an opportunity to acknowledge and support the work of local writers, to bridge the gap between the writers and the community and to encourage and motivate new writers.

Traditionally the reception committee is made up of five members plus the staff at the host library. Planning for the event begins in January. Three members of the committee are members of the African American Librarians Association of Western New York (AALAWNY). Their responsibilities include creating a list of writers for the current year and writing an invitation letter to all of the authors and their guests. Publicity letters are sent to newspapers, media and any special contacts. AALAWNY members arrange for a master of ceremonies, prepare program handouts and introduce participants.

Other committee members locate and secure sponsors/donors with a requesting letter and follow-up call. They plan the menu, pick up the food and arrange the tables. For each of the six past years, a local supermarket has graciously donated refreshments for the event. Five hundred publicity flyers are created, printed and distributed to branch libraries, newspapers and the media. A special display of the authors' published works is arranged with an accompanying list of library holdings.

Enjoying the African American Writers' Reception, April 23, 1998
Left to right: Sharon Holley, Buffalo & Erie County P. L., Charlotte Blake-Alston,
William A. Miles, Assistant Deputy Director, Buffalo & Erie County P.L.,
Karima Amin, and Jean Harvey-Hilton

Speakers include published and aspiring authors. They are young and old, men and women, and most are native Buffalonians. The reception is a wonderful opportunity for these playwrights, novelists, poets, essayists, short story and non-fiction authors to network and share their ideas. Among the many writers have been Dr. Catherine Collins, Buffalo State College professor and author of *Imprisonment of the African Women* and Malik Rasul Bey author of *You Must Inhale to Exhale* and editor of the book, *Intoxicated by the Lynx*. Karima Amin, a favorite local storyteller and author of *You Can Say that Again* and *The Adventures of Brer Rabbit and Friends* is a frequent participant. Each speaker is given a few minutes to discuss his work, his struggles to be published, his failures and successes. Many thank the library for our commitment to this unique and important event. Several have touched on how important it is for them to bring the African American story to children and to give it to them via the printed page. One young writer, inspired by what she heard one year, came back the next year with a published work.

The African American Writers' Reception began as a program of the AALAWNY in 1995. The purpose of the Association is to give back to the community and honor minority writers in Western New York. The reception has always been held at the Martin Luther King Branch Library in Buffalo. Although the event has grown, with nearly 100 people attending, the small community library setting is still conducive to its purpose. People of all ages attend the reception, from aspiring school age children to well-seasoned active individuals. MLK Branch is convenient to public transportation and is wheelchair accessible. The invitations state that the event runs from 5:30 to 8:00 P.M., but people have been so enthusiastic that they come early and stay past 9:00 P.M. Even though our sponsor provides a beautiful display of food, that is not the main draw. People are excited about the opportunity to meet their colleagues and network among themselves.

The entire evening is fun, inspiring and a terrific National Library Week Event. It is a celebration of authors who are committed to the community and to writing. The library continues to encourage more and more people to become involved, share their talents and enjoy this special evening.

INTEGRATING THE MELTING POT

THE UNIVERSITY AT BUFFALO LIBRARIES' Rx FOR DIVERSITY

BY GLENDORA JOHNSON-COOPER

The University Libraries of the University at Buffalo (UB) have been managing a library internship/residency program targeted at underrepresented populations since 1992. The need for greater diversity within the UB Libraries, as well as the profession, convinced us that we needed to craft a solution that would work toward improving racial diversity on both the local and national level. We knew the situation called for us to be proactive.

Library literature documented the underrepresentation of librarians of color in general and particularly within academic institutions. The 1991 *Academic and Public Librarians Data by Race, Ethnicity, and Sex*, compiled by the American Library Association's (ALA) Office for Library Personnel Resources, reported that African Americans represented 4.96 percent of academic librarians (total 486). Hispanics represented 1.53 percent (total 150), Asian/Pacific Islanders represented 4.95 percent (total 485), and American Indian/Alaskan Natives represented .63 percent (total 62).

America's shifting demographics also spoke to the urgency of recruiting more individuals from diverse racial groups to provide culturally sensitive services to the growing multicultural populations. The challenge was overwhelmingly clear to the University Libraries. We needed to make a commitment to increase the numbers of underrepresented groups. We needed to get to work right away. We did what some would think of as unconscionable; we implemented and planned simultaneously, a challenge for sure.

Through a series of meetings and planning sessions led by Associate Vice President for University Libraries, Barbara von Wahlde, a team of librarians and administrators identified specific goals our diversity initiative would seek to address. The planning group included the Human Resources Officer, Kenneth Hood; our Associate Director, Stephen Roberts; and the director of the Undergraduate Library, Margaret Wells. Glendora Johnson-Cooper was appointed Program Manager. Everyone agreed that the Undergraduate Library (UGL) was the logical place to house the program. While these individuals served as the initial planning team, once underway, the effort involved the cooperation of the entire staff of the University Libraries. The primary objectives of the program were to:

- competitively attract dynamic, diverse underrepresented talent to pursue the M.L.S.
- mentor interns/residents and assist with the development of a professional network
- provide a broad introduction to academic librarianship
- assist residents in securing permanent, post-residency employment
- increase the professional output of underrepresented librarians by requiring the completion of a scholarly article
- provide an overview of the tenure process
- provide opportunities for technology training and for integration of new technologies into library instruction and outreach
- provide a welcoming, nurturing environment with opportunities for continuous learning.

The program has evolved since its inception, but the challenge remains to design a learning experience that continuously supports these objectives.

The Library Internship/Residency Program is structured as a three-year program offering a combination of academic training and work experience. Participants gain both a practical and theoretical overview of academic librarianship. The first year is spent pursuing the Master of Library Science degree (M.L.S.) at UB's School of Information Studies (SIS). The intern receives a New York State, Arthur A. Schomburg Graduate Fellowship, which covers tuition and provides an annual stipend of ten thousand dollars. Upon completion of the degree, the intern becomes a resident and begins a two-year position as Visiting Assistant Librarian in the Oscar A. Silverman Undergraduate Library (UGL). The position offers a competitive, entry-level salary plus travel expenses and generous benefits. Resident librarian responsibilities are identical to the responsibilities any entry-level librarian would be assigned. They include providing reference services utilizing print and electronic resources; teaching library instruction classes and Web/Internet workshops; selecting materials for the libraries' collections; writing a scholarly article for publication; participating in professional associations; and completing special projects reflecting each resident's professional interests.

An attractive component of the program is the mentoring which is provided throughout the three years and beyond. Support of travel to professional association meetings helps residents identify external mentors and additional opportunities for professional growth. Residents also establish professional relationships with the entire University Libraries' faculty and staff as well as other University faculty and professionals through various work assignments.

The program is distinguished by its full commitment to identifying a permanent faculty position within an academic library at the conclusion of the three-year appointment. The completion of a scholarly article and the articulation of a statement of research interests strengthen residents' entry into the professional job market. Close mentoring, counseling and the creation of a five-year professional development plan helps residents identify the resources needed to make possible the transition to their "ideal" position. Residents also have the option of and are encouraged to apply for any faculty or professional positions that interest them within the University Libraries.

When operating at full capacity, the program accommodates three individuals—an intern who is pursuing the M.L.S., and a first- and second-year resident. Timing a resident's departure can be tricky and can sometimes shorten the third and final year of the program.

One of our early challenges was to identify interested partners who would join us in our long-term commitment to racial diversity. The program would not be possible without the input and generous support of our partners including the Office of the Vice President for Student Affairs, which contributes one salary line to the program. The Office of the Vice President for Public Service and Urban Affairs annually underwrites support for the pursuit of the M.L.S. through contributing an Arthur A. Schomburg Fellowship. Finally, the School of Information Studies works cooperatively with the Program Manager to identify qualified, accepted candidates for the M.L.S. program.

The Internship/Residency Program is quite rigorous and requires exceptional talents. Ideal candidates should possess a variety of professional and personal characteristics such as flexibility, self-motivation, self-confidence, creativity, leadership potential, reliability, assertiveness, tact, and ability to solve problems. Eligible candidates must:

- have a baccalaureate degree
- commit to completing the M.L.S. within one year at the University at Buffalo
- be a member of one of the following underrepresented groups as defined by SUNY (State University of New York): African American, Hispanic American, Native American
- have an undergraduate GPA of 3.0 (B) or higher

- be a native-born or naturalized U.S. citizen
- be accepted into the UB School of Information Studies
- have the ability to work in a team environment
- have strong oral and written communication skills.

Priority is given to individuals pursuing a first master's degree. In selecting individuals to participate in the program, an advisory committee composed of librarians, UB faculty, graduate students, current residents and administrators considers the following criteria:

- commitment to a career in academic librarianship
- strong written and oral communication skills
- sense of enthusiasm, curiosity, and adaptability to change
- sense of self-direction and self-motivation
- professional maturity and leadership potential.

Finalists are invited to an on-campus interview at the expense of the Libraries.

The Library Internship/Residency Program has evolved into a stellar recruitment effort of which we are quite proud. It offers a supportive, directed opportunity to enter the field of academic librarianship. Since its inception, seventeen individuals have been associated with the program. As might be expected, some have chosen library careers other than academic, including law librarian and school media specialist. Some have chosen not to complete the program for personal reasons. Some residents have moved on and kept no contact. Other residents maintain contact and keep us updated on their professional progress. Residents have gone on to diverse positions across the country. Alysse Jordan is the Social Work Librarian in the Lehman Library at Columbia University. Miguel Juarez is the Art and Architecture Librarian at the University of Arizona at Tucson. Musa Abdul Hakim is a Reference/Instruction Librarian at the State University College at Buffalo. Eric Acree is Instruction Coordinator at the Oscar A. Silverman Undergraduate Library at the University at Buffalo. Portia Diaz-Martin is a Reference/Electronic Services Librarian at Indiana University of Pennsylvania.

We clearly look forward to expanding our numbers and working toward the day when special recruitment efforts such as the Library Internship/Residency Program are no longer needed. The program has come a long way and still faces many interesting challenges including:

- the need for increased publicity, both internally and externally
- increased funding to expand the number of participants
- closer linkages with other residency programs
- increased opportunities for specialization within the UB Libraries
- better outcome assessment and post-residency follow-up
- identification of ways to standardize program procedures in the interest of more efficient program management.

Managing a residency program is just one way to begin increasing the number of underrepresented ethnic groups in the profession. It is a labor-intensive effort requiring a serious commitment to the profession and a willingness to respond to the rigors of mentoring. It is tough but rewarding work that more libraries should consider undertaking. The more institutions that undertake the challenge, the sooner we will remedy the shortage of librarians of color.

TRIBUTE TO DR. MARTIN LUTHER KING JR.

By Suzanne Jacobs

The dream continues. This year's twenty-second annual "Tribute to Dr. Martin Luther King Jr." at the Buffalo & Erie County Public Library continued the celebration of cultural diversity and freedom. Year after year this tribute has sparked community involvement and participation. The goal of this project is not only to honor Dr. King, his words and works, but also to bring unity and inspiration to the city of Buffalo.

A sixteen-member committee, which has grown throughout the years, meets in August to begin brainstorming for the upcoming program in January. Each year the committee establishes a new theme for the program, giving it a fresh look and purpose. Past themes include, "Unity in the Community", "Lift Every Voice and Sing" and "Living the Dream Together." There is always much work to be done including making community contacts, locating sponsors, creating publicity, and technical planning.

Each year schoolchildren are invited to participate in a unique way. Recent contests included an essay in which children were asked to write about a person in their life who has inspired them and what they feel that person has contributed to the world. Several years ago children had fun creating poems and rap songs, and then presenting them to the audience. Children have displayed their art abilities with a bookmark, which they created for the library. In addition, children from city schools have showcased their talent during the program through song, readings and dance. In 1994, a group called "Singing Hands" presented *America the Beau-*

tiful in American Sign Language. Children at School 53 have traditionally participated yearly in this event, arriving in busloads accompanied by their parents. Children have always been eager to be a part of the celebration.

My feet Is realtired but my Soul Is rested "

Winner of Bookmark Design Contest sponsored by Buffalo & Erie County P.L., Dept. of Extension Services as part of the Tribute to Dr. Martin Luther King Jr. held on January 19, 1999. Bookmark designed by Brody Mull, 2nd Grade

Many of our city's leaders, including television personalities and politicians, have volunteered their time to offer their talents as role models for the community. Majority Leader of the Erie County Legislature, Crystal Peoples, has dedicated herself to improving the partnership of the public library system and cultural organizations with the inner city community. Well-known anchorpeople on the local news channels have been favorite participants in the event. Other church and civic leaders have added their perspectives to the tribute throughout the years. Each of the masters of ceremonies and/or keynote speakers has thoughtfully expressed personal insights on our role in preserving Dr. King's memory.

Young people who participate in the event and have been finalists in the contest have been awarded certificates of recognition. The committee has also solicited potential sponsors for donations of gift certificates to present to the contest winners. We have been fortunate to have generous sponsors provide all funding for the event.

Technical aspects of the event require careful consideration. Committee members have become stagehands the night of the show, juggling lights, curtain and microphones. Groups also have to be quietly directed on and off the stage. The event has been videotaped for later enjoyment. No major mishaps have ever taken place because of good planning and practice.

Publicity is distributed at library branches, to schools and through community and city newspapers. When the program began in 1978, it was held in the county's Martin Luther King Branch Library. As the years went by and the event grew, it was moved to the Central Library's auditorium. For the past several years it has taken place in late January on a Thursday evening, but now few people remain downtown at night during the winter. The committee has discussed moving the event to daytime to enable more schoolchildren to participate. The tribute has been our traditional event for the last twenty-two years.

Preparation has already begun for the 2001 Tribute to Dr. King. Looking back at the event's growing success, we are confident that this program will continue to add strength and a renewed spirit to our community.

CANANDAIGUA

CULTURAL CONNECTIONS AND BEYOND

By Patricia Stocker

Pioneer Library System provides services to forty-two member libraries and seven correctional facilities in a four-county rural area (Livingston, Ontario, Wayne and Wyoming) in upstate New York. This article focuses on a Library Services and Technology Act (LSTA) project entitled "Cultural Connections" that took place during 1992–1994, and dicusses what has happened since the federal funding ended.

The 1990 census revealed that 97 percent of those living in the Pioneer Library System service area were white, 2 percent were African American, and 1 percent were Hispanic or other ethnic groups. When "Cultural Connections" was first funded in 1992 there were very few Spanish language materials available in any of the member libraries. Library services and programming to the Hispanic community were practically non-existent. And although 35 percent of the total number of individuals of Hispanic origin living in Pioneer's service area were incarcerated in one of the seven prisons, most of the correctional facilities had limited amounts of Spanish language materials.

During the first year of funding eight rotating collections of Spanish language materials were developed and placed in six member libraries and two prison libraries. The second year of funding, two more rotating collections were added, for a total of ten. A core collection of approximately 500 Spanish language items was selected for Geneva Free Library, Pioneer's Central Library.

Over the course of the two-year grant period nearly 1,500 Spanish language materials were acquired. A union list and videography of the materials was compiled and shared with member libraries. Spanish language registration cards were distributed to members. Press releases and public service announcements were produced and sent to appropriate media contacts.

A Caribbean rhythm and movement group, Salmorejo, presented programs to help introduce the new Spanish language materials. The library-sponsored programs took place in a community center, a farm market, at a community festival, and of course, at libraries. One of the accomplishments of this project was the heightened cultural awareness and sensitivity that occurred because of the performances of Salmorejo. More than one library reported that members of their community thanked them for providing culturally diverse programming.

Another component of the grant was the presentation of a workshop for librarians. Entitled "Cultural Diversity: Opening Doors", the workshop featured presenters who led interactive activities, which allowed for the examination of barriers and supports to the full celebration of all differences (ethnicity, race, religion, sexual preference, ability, class and gender). A special focus was given to issues of race relations relevant to Latino/a cultures in predominantly white communities. A luncheon of *arroz con gandules, ensalada, plátanos, pollo con especias, pan y mantequilla, postres* and *ponche* – rice with pigeon peas, salad, plantains, spicy chicken, bread and butter, desserts, and punch – was served to over forty who attended the workshop.

What has happened since 1994 when the federal funding of the "Cultural Connections" project came to an end?

- Pioneer's outreach and AV departments and Geneva Free Library have made a concerted effort to add Spanish language materials to both the rotating collections and to the Central Library collection.

- Additional grant funding has been actively sought and received and monies have been set aside from the outreach operating budget to add new materials on a regular basis.

- Spanish language rotating collections of books and videos have been designed exclusively for the correctional facilities, with half of the prisons participating in this program.

- An Adult Literacy Service grant administered by the Central Library in 1999–2000 has reached out to the Geneva Hispanic community to offer literacy programs and services.

- The Grolier Spanish language encyclopedia *Nueva enciclopedia Cumbre en línea* is available online on the Pioneer Library Web site.

- The Gates Foundation initiative will provide computers with Spanish language software installed for five member libraries.

- An innovative Even Start Family Literacy program that will reach migrant farmworker families began in September 2000.

Let me tell you a bit about this last item, which is our latest project. Mobile Even Start is a program that partners the Pioneer Library System, Genesee–Valley BOCES (Geneseo Migrant Program) and the New York State Federation of Growers and Processors, Inc. (Agri-Business Child Development). This New York State Education Department Title I Part B Even Start Family Literacy-funded project began in September 2000 and is expected to continue for a four-year period.

Living in remote geographical locations, frequently lacking transportation and working twelve- to fourteen-hour days as dictated by weather and crops, migrant farmworker families face incredible barriers when trying to access educational programs.

Logo designed by Ellen Henrie for the Pioneer Library System's Even Start Program

Typically, even when an educational program exists nearby, families are unable to attend. To overcome these and other obstacles, the proposed program will provide comprehensive family literacy services in migrant camps, homes, and migrant Head Start programs. Family Educators based at Migrant Education Outreach Programs will provide integrated instruction including adult education, early childhood education, parenting education and structured parent-child time.

Pioneer Library System will enrich the literacy possibilities for migrant farmworker families by offering a materials development and training component, yielding culturally- and language-appropriate opportunities.

A part-time Special Projects Librarian has been hired whose first-year goals are to:

• define the need for library service to migrant farmworker families

- gather baseline data regarding current library service to migrant farmworkers in New York State and in other states throughout the country
- develop collections of library materials that will be used by Family Educators and migrant farmworker families
- develop a collection that will include professional titles, parenting, health, recreational and bilingual materials for Pioneer Library System's Central Library, Geneva Free Library
- develop training for Family Educators to teach them how to encourage migrant farmworker families to read to their children, and training for library staff to teach them strategies to reach migrant and other disenfranchised populations.

This unique project will continue to grow and develop over the four-year period. Evaluation will be ongoing and results shared with the library community.

Too often programs fall by the wayside when grant funding comes to an end. This has definitely not been the case with Pioneer. The number of Spanish language materials available system-wide has increased dramatically over the last eight years. Pioneer will continue to seek ways to provide the financial resources needed to supplement these collections.

FLORIDA

BOOKSTART IN SPANISH
COMENZANDO CON LIBROS

BY MADELYN FOLINO

Our community is served by a school district library chartered to serve a population of 4,724 (1990 census) in the Florida Union Free School District in Orange County, New York. The library, organized in 1958, has been housed in various rented quarters for the last forty-two years, most recently a trailer, which was just replaced by a new building in October 2000.

We saw the great need for services to Spanish-speaking residents in Florida, and in August of 1999 offered the first bilingual Bookstart program in New York State. Bookstart, authored by Cornell Cooperative Extension, is designed to introduce the world of children's literature to low literacy parents of young children. In six sessions, parents learn how to choose, use and make books for their children. Discussions focus on examples of children's classics, how books reflect our values and cultures, and how books can be used to start conversations on a wide variety of issues.

In the course of offering a Bookstart program to our community in July, 1999, we were approached by Florida Agri-Business Child Development (ABCD), a local agency which provides childcare for the children of migrant farmworkers in the Black Dirt region of Orange County. Staff members at ABCD were interested in Bookstart and thought that Spanish-speaking parents would be, too. Fortunately, the Ramapo–Catskill Library System (RCLS), which had secured the grant funding for Bookstart, had money for one additional program.

Planning proceeded rapidly over the course of two weeks. Educator Denyse Variano of Cornell Cooperative Extension, a veteran Bookstart facilitator, volunteered to share leadership of the group with me. My confidence about planning a bilingual program was buoyed by the library's successful July program, my past experience as a teacher for the Mid-Hudson Summer Migrant Education Outreach Program and by my experience as a storyteller for many years. ABCD Education Coordinator Tim Hill volunteered to interpret at every session and to translate publicity and Bookstart materials into Spanish. Translations were reviewed and discussed for accuracy and ease of comprehension by native Spanish speakers from various countries. A key component of the program was transportation, arranged by ABCD, and childcare, which was provided by local Girl Scouts. Our Friends of the Library group provided refreshments and our friends at the Farmworkers Community Alliance spread the word about the program.

We were under pressure to meet the grant's September deadline and schedule the program during the few hours and months when seasonal workers could attend, so the decision was made to meet Monday–Friday, August 16–20, 7:00–9:00 P.M., rather than in weekly sessions. The program was advertised in both languages through flyers handed directly to the parents. All materials were created at the library and translated by ABCD.

Randall Enos, RCLS Children's Services Consultant, helped us tremendously by expediting the ordering and delivery of free books for the parents, arts and crafts materials, puppets and toys, and one thousand dollars worth of books for the library, all funded by the grant he had written. We created a juvenile collection of Spanish and Spanish/English books, choosing to order, when available, Spanish versions of the books we had received for our first Bookstart. Thus, we were able to read aloud, discuss and circulate wonderful, brand new stories in both languages. It was challenging to find a good selection of titles in Spanish in our limited planning time and we relied mainly on Brodart Library Supplies & Furnishings to supply the books.

The group met in a classroom at ABCD, a familiar place for parents and children. Attendance varied between ten and seventeen parents and teachers each evening. The need to say everything twice—in English and Spanish—slowed the pace a bit, but also allowed much participation and many laughs to ensure that we really were "on the same page." Some parents were quite reserved until we demonstrated finger plays and puppets. Suddenly, their shyness was forgotten as they shared favorite childhood rhymes from Mexico, Chile and El Salvador. We discovered many similar themes and came to appreciate the difficulty of translating our beloved Mother Goose! Lively discussions were held on which books were suitable for babies, toddlers, preschoolers and beginning readers.

For many of the migrant parents, the books provided for the program, whether in English or Spanish, were the first books they had ever taken home. No participants were fluent or literate in both languages, so having a variety of books and taking the time to translate hand-outs, spoken presentations and discussions was vital in engaging the group. Participants eagerly made books for their children from luggage tags and stickers and reported their experiences, many having shared a book with a child for the first time.

Our program ended on Friday evening, with a visit to the library (also a first for many) and included a tour of the various collections, the circulation desk, and information on how to apply for a library card. We shared our favorite books and acted out a story with puppets. In September, the library and ABCD sponsored a fiesta for parents from both summer Bookstarts. We used English, Spanish, pantomime, and some high school French, to communicate our knowledge of books, storytelling and the library. Each parent received four books to take home.

The library has continued its outreach to the migrant community through storytimes and the summer reading program. Our Spanish collection is a great asset and a prize for a library of our small size. I feel that our creation of "Comenzando con libros" was a successful model for inter-agency collaboration and an effective program in reaching an overlooked and underserved population, hungry for the nourishment that only stories and storytelling can bring. In October 2000, we were awarded the Ramapo–Catskill Library System's Program of the Year Award for "Comenzando con libros."

In May 2000 we applied to the New York State Division of Library Development for an adult literacy grant to offer tutor training by Literacy Volunteers of America; establish a collection of easy reading materials for adults; and promote the use of the library as a tutoring site, especially for migrant workers. We received more money than we had asked for! As of June 2001, ten tutors have been trained and the library has promoted many matches with migrant farmworkers interested in learning to read English. A second successful bilingual Bookstart program was offered in July 2001 and has led to another new adventure in outreach—computer instruction in Spanish. These experiences prove to me that a good idea, enthusiasm and teamwork, plus funding, even of a modest amount, are the real ingredients needed for successful programs.

GLENS FALLS

SISTER LIBRARIES
CRANDALL PUBLIC LIBRARY, GLENS FALLS, NEW YORK
AND THE SAGA CITY MUNICIPAL LIBRARY, SAGA CITY, JAPAN
—AND BEYOND

By Christine McDonald

The path to becoming a sister library for Crandall Public Library began in the early 1990s with meetings with the Common Council of Glens Falls. The council wanted to find a place to exhibit and store memorabilia and gifts from visits to Saga City, Japan, Glens Falls' sister city. Glens Falls, New York and Saga City, Japan established a Sister Cities relationship in 1988 based upon mutual interest in hot air balloons. Both communities host hot air balloon festivals each year with balloon teams from Glens Falls traveling to Saga and vice versa as the first link the two communities had to strengthen ties as Sister Cities. Crandall Public Library's relationship with the Saga City Municipal Library in Japan began in 1995. In that year, Crandall Public Library established a permanent exhibit of the fine arts, folk arts and local crafts from the Saga City area. Saga is known as the only place in the world where silk and silver embroidery is produced and examples of this fine work were given a permanent home at Crandall. Saga is also known for fine porcelain, many examples of which are also on display.

At the invitation of the mayor of Saga City, I traveled in 1996 with a Sister City delegation to Saga City, Japan to celebrate the opening of the new 238,000 square foot public library, the Saga City Municipal Library. Along with the Mayor of Glens Falls, I participated in the opening of the new facility. The two libraries signed a Treaty of Cooperation as Sister Libraries on August 8, 1996. The Mayor of Glens Falls, Vince De Santis, and I signed the treaty for Crandall Public Library and Mayor Nishimura and

Chief Librarian Chiba Osamu of Saga City signed for Saga City. All signers were asked to speak to those present with translators assisting in delivering the messages of cooperation and future collaborations. It was a great privilege to address the Saga community. I was unaccustomed to being treated with such honor and was especially pleased when the women in the audience gave me a standing ovation because, as they told me later, I was a female manager, a rarity in Japan. At the ceremony, I presented books related to the region served by Crandall, namely the Adirondack Mountains of New York State, which are within the library's service area. Wordless picture books, other children's books, a reproduction of an oil painting of Crandall Public Library and a delightful primitive folk art print of the library depicted as the "Heart of the Community" were also presented to our Saga colleagues. The Saga City Librarian presented Crandall Public Library with books and videos on Japan and Saga City, and porcelain from local artists.

Mayor Vincent De Santis, Glens Falls, N.Y., and Library Director Christine McDonald, Crandall P.L. signing the Sister Library Agreement in Saga City, Japan establishing the Glens Falls–Saga City Library Relationship

Maintaining the sister library relationship has been facilitated by yearly visits between the cities. Because of the Sister City relationship, many links have been developed in both communities with the community college educators and students, Tae Kwon Do instructors, balloon teams, high school students and teachers and librarians. Delegates from both communities always visit the two libraries during the yearly visits as a regular itinerary stop. Crandall and Saga City continue to exchange materials, which are catalogued and circulated. Saga City produces a newsletter in English about Sister City activities, which is available at Crandall for the community and for people interested in joining a delegation to Saga. During the spring and summer of 2000, Crandall had an exhibition of student artwork from several grade schools and high schools in Saga City. Many of the Saga City artists included pictures of themselves and a short biography. In May of 2000, a student delegation from Saga City toured the library and they were pleased and delighted to see the artwork of friends back in Saga on display.

In 1999, Crandall Public Library and the City of Glens Falls along with the Saga City Municipal Library and the City of Saga, Japan were selected to be NCLIS Sister Libraries. The program was developed by the National Commission on Library and Information Science, an independent agency of the federal government, as part of the White House Millennium Council Project for the year 2000. Crandall Public Library plans to expand the relationship with our sister library through other meaningful exchanges in the future.

My interest in sister libraries came from having lived overseas several times in the past. In my early twenties, I lived and worked as a Peace Corps volunteer in a remote part of southern Chile. The small town I called home was Puerto Natales, which is located in the Chilean part of Patagonia. It was there that I experienced a community without a public library. The impact on my life was enormous. Although I treasure every moment that I spent in Chile, it was difficult on a day-to-day basis to live without a library nearby. One had to rely on friends to send reading material or the small stationery store with a few books that was the only source of books in my small village. The closest bookstore was in Punta Arenas, four hours south by bus on a dirt highway. News came via radio for television had not yet arrived in Patagonia. Since then, I have never taken the privilege of having a public library in one's community for granted. Living in another country also taught me the valuable lesson that I could learn from the people of other cultures who approached life and the world differently from me.

When I was in Japan, I was fortunate enough to have a caring host family—a husband and wife and their eight-year-old son. The wife worked as a teacher's aide and also volunteered at the library. They asked what I wanted to see while I was in Kyushu Province and were interested that my only request was to see Nagasaki. My host mother remarked that her son had also expressed a desire to see the museum of the atomic bombing and the Peace Memorial in Nagasaki. A bustling town nestled in beautiful green hills, Nagasaki reminded me of San Francisco. As I pondered the destruction of Nagasaki, I made connections with my father's ordeal at Pearl Harbor in 1941 and my uncle's death in a submarine off the coast of Japan in 1944. My links to Japan were strong. What had ultimately brought me to Japan was my career as a librarian and my commitment to the sister library program. That day with my host family was memorable. After touring the museum and visiting the Peace Memorial, we had lunch in Nagasaki's Chinatown. In the streets of Nagasaki, among the older residents, I did catch a glimpse of an old woman whose face had been deformed by the bomb. The discussions we had that day were difficult and will remain embedded in my memory forever. We each confronted our own interpretations of those tragic events, agreeing and disagreeing with respect and restraint.

I know that thousands of librarians have had experiences in their travels that would make them sympathetic to the idea of developing a sister library relationship. Many librarians serve populations whose first language is not English and whose cultures bring great depth to their communities. So many of our patrons now come from other countries and their experiences and perspectives add to our understanding of the world community. From my experience, it is the personal that motivates us to consider becoming a sister library with a library in another country. Many New York State libraries have become NCLIS Sister Libraries. There are countless opportunities available for librarians to get involved as sister libraries. So many of us in the U.S. have relatives who were born in another country. Many of us travel and meet colleagues abroad. Some of us attend the conferences of the International Federation of Library Associations and Institutions (IFLA).

In 1998, while I was attending an orientation session for new Public Library Association board members in Chicago, the incoming President of the American Library Association (ALA), Sarah Long, was pitching her ideas about sister libraries. Briefly, I mentioned our sister library relationship with Saga City and followed up with a detailed letter about it. As a result of that letter, she asked me to chair the Sister Library Initiative Committee and I accepted. The first meeting of the committee was held at ALA's Midwinter Conference in Philadelphia. Sarah outlined what she wished to accomplish with the Sister Library program, which officially began at the ALA Midwinter 2000 Meeting in San Antonio. The Sister Library Committee developed a tip sheet in English for librarians interested in starting a sister library relationship. The tip sheet was included in the October 1999 issue of *American Libraries*. Another tip sheet was translated into Spanish specifically for the ALA San Antonio meeting and for the Guadalajara (Mexico) Book Fair. Both tip sheets were aimed at assisting libraries in finding a sister library and in setting up a meaningful relationship with levels of commitment suitable to each library's goals and objectives as a sister library. In fact, there have been success stories of libraries that have linked up with other libraries in an informal sister library relationship. Some have built on their sister city relationships and others have become NCLIS sister libraries. The tip sheet suggests that libraries contact a list of international organizations to assist them in finding a sister library partner. For libraries that cannot afford to travel to their sister library, information about each sister library can be mounted on each of the library's web pages. For large urban libraries, having more than one sister library might fulfill their needs in providing for cultural exchanges for many populations.

In January 2000 at the ALA Midwinter Conference in San Antonio, Texas, library leaders from Latin America were invited to attend to discuss library services in the new millennium with library leaders from the U.S. This meeting was an important opportunity to build upon relationships with our neighbors in Latin America and to establish sister library relationships throughout the hemisphere. As Sarah Long's presidency was coming to a close, I began to search for a home for the Sister Library Committee. Having worked closely with ALA's International Relations Office, I looked to the International Relations Round Table (IRRT) to take on a new subcommittee. I made my request to IRRT to become a subcommittee and they agreed to confer this status on the Sister Library Committee. This committee will continue the work of the first committee and plan for the future. In 2001, at the ALA Midwinter Conference, the committee started to set up the structure of working committees to assist in promoting the sister library concept and to assist libraries of all types in finding a partner. The International Relations Office of ALA assists IRRT committees in their work.

Currently, I am working on a new sister library project. For the past three years I have been going to Guatemala as a Spanish translator, with a local medical team that provides health care to residents of the province of Santa Rosa. As a librarian, I noticed that there was no public library and I spoke to our host in Guatemala, the local Lions Club coordinator of the medical project. I explained my desire to see a public library established. We talked

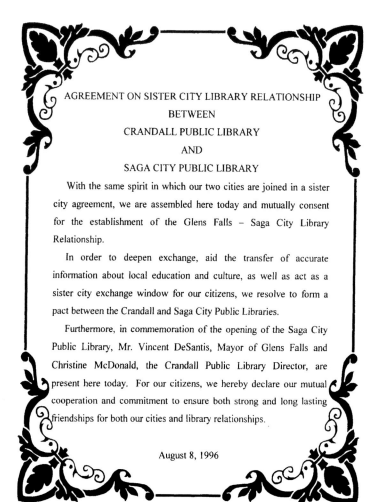

AGREEMENT ON SISTER CITY LIBRARY RELATIONSHIP
BETWEEN
CRANDALL PUBLIC LIBRARY
AND
SAGA CITY PUBLIC LIBRARY

With the same spirit in which our two cities are joined in a sister city agreement, we are assembled here today and mutually consent for the establishment of the Glens Falls – Saga City Library Relationship.

In order to deepen exchange, aid the transfer of accurate information about local education and culture, as well as act as a sister city exchange window for our citizens, we resolve to form a pact between the Crandall and Saga City Public Libraries.

Furthermore, in commemoration of the opening of the Saga City Public Library, Mr. Vincent DeSantis, Mayor of Glens Falls and Christine McDonald, the Crandall Public Library Director, are present here today. For our citizens, we hereby declare our mutual cooperation and commitment to ensure both strong and long lasting friendships for both our cities and library relationships.

August 8, 1996

Facsimile of the "Agreement on Sister City Library Relationship Between Crandall Public Library and Saga City Public Library" and in June 2000, my good friend, Pepe Marien, of the Lions Club in Quilapa, Guatemala, traveled to Glens Falls and brought plans from Guatemala for a new clinic with a public library as part of the small complex. I was able to get very tentative funding commitments from my Rotary Club and the Lions Club in Glens Falls to assist. The library is planned as a small part of the medical clinic, which will be run by volunteers. Ground breaking is planned for 2002–2003 depending upon our mutual success in fund raising. Several local service clubs in my area have expressed interest in buying books for the new library. A university student from Guatemala has agreed to come to Crandall Public Library for about six weeks to receive in-service training in library basics. The Lions Club in Guatemala has agreed to pay her expenses and one of the pediatricians in our community who goes with us each year has agreed to provide housing while she is in the U.S. The student will bring back what she has learned to Santa Rosa province to assist in setting up the library. When the clinic/library opens for business, I hope that my library will become a sister library with our new Guatemalan public library. Knowing that I will be able to travel to Guatemala each year with the medical team and work on the library there is something I look forward to doing in the coming years. Anyone else interested in this project can contact me. We would appreciate any expertise you may wish to offer.

I encourage librarians to continue to explore and make connections with the rich and diverse cultures of the world. If this exploration leads to a sister library relationship, you and your community will be enriched by the experience, whether it lasts one year or a lifetime.

GREENWICH

BLACK HISTORY CELEBRATION

By Claudia Blackler

The community of Greenwich is nestled among the green hills that lie between New York's Hudson River and the Green Mountains of Vermont. Dairy farms and orchards abound in the region. Fishermen from all over the world visit to fish the famous Battenkill River that runs through the town. In winter tourists visit to cross-country ski and downhill ski. In the autumn tourists fill the roads to view the splendor of the foliage.

In addition to the year-round scenic splendor and quiet, close-knit village life, the area offers a well regarded public school system and library. The library was established in 1902, at the urging of a small group of local women who saw the need for a public library. Today our library serves a population of 4,557 people; 2,768 of them are registered patrons. Forty-eight thousand items circulated in 1999. The library operates with a staff of one full time director, a part time assistant, and a clerk who works six hours a week. Thirty-four volunteers manage the circulation desk, bring books to homebound patrons, run story hours, provide homework assistance, keep the shelves in order, manage our history room, and maintain a flower garden, to name just a few of their duties.

An African American patron of the Greenwich Free Library, Cliff Oliver, who is also a noted photographer and recent honoree of the NAACP, had volunteered to preserve the old photographs in our history room. We were very grateful, and when we asked if there might be something we could do in return, he suggested we consider having a celebration in honor of Black History Month. We have a small number of African Americans in Greenwich and surrounding towns, but privately thought that only our families, a few friends, and the speakers would come.

The library staff met one evening about three months before the Black History Month event, which was scheduled for February 9, 2000. Goals were outlined and we decided on speakers to talk about issues and history, a storyteller for the children and a soul food dinner. To attract attention to the event, we wrote a letter and sent it to all the local teachers, politicians, artists, and members of the local Daughters of the American Revolution chapter. Notices were sent to five local and regional newspapers. We sent flyers to local churches and put a notice in the school newsletter that is sent to the students' parents. A final meeting, one month before the program, allowed us to coordinate the responses to our letters and to plan the event in detail.

The library policy is to offer free programs, and since the library was about to undertake a fundraiser to expand facilities, we were asked not to solicit funds. The Board of Trustees gave one hundred dollars, which was used to purchase paper goods, and local stores generously contributed food. Using a cookbook with recipes for fried chicken, greens, corn bread, sweet potato pie, and iced tea, we contacted Friends of the Library, patrons, and community members and asked them if they would prepare the food. As the date grew nearer we started to get feedback from the community. People were excited! Students were to get extra credit for attending the event. We did not panic, but we called for more food to be prepared!

Our library building is small with no place for a community room so we set up tables in the children's and adult sections of the library and we set the food on top of the children's bookshelves covered with linens. We purchased some African print fabric to put on top of the white cloths and decorated the walls with artwork we received from local artist and book illustrator, Donald Cook. He gave us original drawings he had made while working on illustrations depicting images and lives of African Americans.

We put together an exhibit of books and Mr. Oliver's photographs of famous African Americans, which was displayed for the entire month. The event started with the meal and the line slowly moved as people filled their plates, ate, and then made room for more people. By the end, over 140 people had tasted and enjoyed the food! Everyone was in great spirits.

We invited Mr. Tom Cooper, the first executive director of the Martin Luther King Jr. Commission, a past director of the N. Y. S. Martin Luther King Jr. Institute for Non-Violence, and a member of the faculty of the King Center in Atlanta, Georgia. At the time he was in the process of setting up a program, "Aspects of Race and Incarceration" with the N.Y.S. Department of Correctional Services. At our event he discussed issues of slavery in contemporary society. Assistant Vice Chancellor at SUNY/Albany Jacqueline Davis Ohwevwo, who is also a teacher of African Studies, read poems written by African Americans. Mr. Patrick Sorsby of the Society for the Preservation of the Underground Railroad discussed the Underground Railroad in the Hudson and Champlain Valley. Ms. Estella Johnson, a member of the Willard's Mountain Chapter of the Daughters of the American Revolution talked about the involvement of a local resident of Greenwich in the rescue of a free Black man, Solomon Northrup, who had been captured and sold into slavery. This event is known as "The Jerri Rescue." Washington County Historian Joe Cutshall-King talked on how the Washington County census was constructed before 1790. Sweet Mama Stringbean, an African American storyteller, shared some of her stories. Mr. Oliver, along with several other members of the community, presented a video about the local houses that are historically connected to the Underground Railroad.

When the speakers' presentations were over, several members of the audience asked if they could add something. Our local Vocalist/Storyteller, Dr. MaryNell Morgan, entertained us with a song about Harriet Tubman. Then she taught our audience the chorus and soon had the whole room singing. Mr. Richard Babcock, a well-known barn restorer, read his poem, "The Unknown

Slave," and also spoke about how he often uncovers information about slaves that lived in the area while researching barns.

One of the memorable remarks overheard was from a young high school student: "...boy this is great...a chicken dinner, and extra credit..." And many other people commented that this was their very first visit to the library.

The Board of Trustees of the library remarked that it was the best and most well-attended program ever held at the library. One member said it was a real "happening"! The person we hired to manage our fundraising campaign was thrilled at the goodwill that was generated by this program. It also was made apparent to the community that the library does indeed need more space. We wrote our own review about the event and sent it to the local newspapers.

Next year we plan to have the same event, maybe with some minor changes. There will still be no charge. We will develop a series of programs to be held after school for students as well as pre-school storyhours, and will reserve spaces for adults 16 and over. We hope to have Cliff Oliver do a re-enactment of the Solomon Northrup story.

Greenwich is rich in the history of the Underground Railroad, which is undocumented except by stories passed down through families. As a result of this program, townspeople have become interested in researching this information. We have obtained a copy of the list of Black men from Greenwich who received land grants from Gerrit Smith between the years of 1846 and 1855, which enabled them to vote. We are now working with high school students from Greenwich and African American students from the Albany Boys Club to find out what happened to these people. We will host all of these students for a weekend during Black History Month. The weekend program will include the planned re-enactment, a walking tour of Underground Railroad sites, and cross-country skiing at a local farm.

By introducing our community to various topics of Black history we spark patrons' interest in this important part of the history of Greenwich which has too often been ignored...until now!

GUILDERLAND

DUTCH HERITAGE WEEK
NOVEMBER 9–14, 1998

BY DOROTHY HOLT

The Guilderland Public Library brought Dutch heritage to life by sponsoring a week of multimedia programs to commemorate Dutch-American Heritage Day, November 16. A 1998 summer performance by the Frisian folk group, Kat yn' t Seil, and a Summer Reading Club Program, entitled "Hunt for History," re-awakened our awareness of Guilderland's Dutch heritage. Inspired by the success of these programs, we decided to explore more deeply the aspects of Dutch culture in the region. The library scheduled Dutch Heritage Week for November 9–14 and we invited cultural historians, scholars, teachers, culinary experts and musicians to participate in our celebration.

'Guilderland' is a corruption of the name of the Dutch province Gelderland, so the event had a special significance for the library's immediate community, though it was also meaningful to all the inhabitants of the Capital Region. Because of the way Americans learn history, they assume that colonial history was dominated by the British: the Mayflower and the Pilgrims in New England; the Gardiner family and other noble English families on Long Island; and Capt. John Smith and James Edward Oglethorpe in the southern colonies. However, the Dutch were the first Europeans to successfully settle in North America, arriving eleven years before the Pilgrims had landed in Plymouth, Massachusetts. New Netherland included all or parts of present-day Delaware, New Jersey and New York, stretching from the Delaware River and Chesapeake Bay on the south to New York City and the Hudson Valley in the north.

Our intention was to explain the region's Dutch heritage and its history going back to the seventeenth century. But as the event developed, participants realized that the Dutch experience with the problems of adapting to an unfamiliar environment, negotiating with native peoples and administering a diverse population of Dutch, religious refugees, and African Americans foreshadowed the challenges and opportunities of multicultural American society in the late twentieth century.

Program details

Our first program opened with a presentation by Mr. Everett Rau, a historian of Dutch barns and colonial agriculture. He described Dutch barn design concepts and details so vividly that even people with no interest in barns were intrigued. Mr. Rau used a wooden model of a Dutch barn — about four feet long, three feet wide and two feet high — and an array of tools and artifacts to explain pre-colonial farming vocabulary and operations. The program was scheduled for an hour, but his congenial, informed style prompted many questions and extended conversations after the program. Mr. Rau allowed us to display his Dutch Barn model for a month afterward and it inspired curiosity in many of our patrons.

Tuesday evening, November 10th, we showed a film produced by the Acorn Foundation (New York City, NY), "Under Two Flags: Colonial New York, 1609–1783," a documentary film which focuses on the important contributions of the Dutch settlers in New Netherland/New York.

On Wednesday, November 11th, we scheduled two afternoon programs to take advantage of Veterans Day, a school holiday for the children. Mr. Owen Colfer presented "Milestones in Guilderland's History through Song," which included such songs as "The Pine Bush Barren's Karner Butterfly Blues" and his newest creation "John Schoolcraft's Lament." Mr. Colfer has been a pioneer in the movement to introduce the community into the curriculum and is the author of *Guilderland: Town Along the Turnpike.*

Everett Rau with his Dutch barn model featured in Guilderland P. L.'s
Dutch Heritage Week celebration, November 1998

Following Mr. Colfer's presentation, Ms. Yanny Venema from the New Netherland Project of the New York State Library, brought in an architectural diorama of a street in 'Beverwyck', the Dutch name for Albany, based on seventeenth century Dutch documents. Ms. Venema provided the children and adult audience with a hands-on presentation that included a discussion of "the butcher, the baker, the candle-stick maker" and where they might have resided.

On the evening of November 11th, Ms. Peter G. Rose gave a lecture and slide show entitled "The Influence of the Dutch on the American Kitchen." Ms. Rose, a nationally recognized food writer and historian from the Netherlands, is the author of *Foods of the Hudson,* and the editor and translator (from the Dutch) of *The Sensible Cook: Dutch Foodways in the Old and the New World.* Her articles have been published in various periodicals including *The New York Times*.

After each program we served food ordered from Vander Veen's Dutch Store, an importing company in Grand Rapids, Michigan. *Stroopwafels* and many other foods, which had appeared in Rose's slides of paintings by the artist Jan Steen, were served, adding an element of delicious excitement to the programs. Also served were *smeerkaas* (cheese spread), *cervelaatworst* (beef sausage), smoked *makreel* (eel) and *paling* (herring).

Thursday evening, November 12th, Mr. Stefan Bielinski, founder and director of the Colonial Albany Social History Project at the New York State Museum, presented "Meet the People of Colonial Albany," a multimedia program. "Albany: A Song of Community," an original work composed by Mr. Bielinski for Albany's tercentennial, accompanied an engaging slide show. The program covered Albany history from the arrival of the Dutch in the early seventeenth century to the early twentieth century, and explained the Dutch contribution to local society. It offered good insights on the friction and co-existence between the Dutch and the English who arrived after them.

Our week-long festivities culminated in a program of Dutch games for children organized and directed by Ms. Anneke Bull, Dutch historian, lecturer and performer who spent three hours with over fifty children, teaching them several different games, such as 'Sjoelen,' a slide game, and 'Mansergernea' (Don't Get Caught), a Dutch board game.

After Dutch Heritage Week was over, the response from the community was overwhelming: I received many phone calls with favorable comments and inquiries about the food, performers and games.

We publicized the events using feature articles, entertainment listings, newsletter articles in *Kids, etc.* (our Youth Services newsletter) and in our regular library newsletter. Notices were sent home with Guilderland's schoolchildren. Ms. Julia Fuentes, our resident graphic artist and library clerk, produced outstanding flyers and brochures. I contacted the speakers and arranged the taste-tempting Dutch treats and Youth Services Department Head Cherry Neil gave all of us the support and time to do it well.

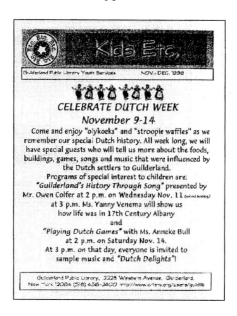

**Children's Services newsletter advertising Dutch Heritage Week activities
Guilderland P.L., November 1998**

The Dutch Heritage Week encouraged participants to look deeper into local history and enjoy the unexpected insights and discoveries that resulted. Although the program emphasized Dutch history and culture, speakers reinforced the point that every heritage has something unique and valuable if you take the time to look for it. An amazing array of copies of historic documents, including county records and song sheets, was handed out by various speakers and added to the educational value of the program.

This program won Outstanding Program of the Year Award for 1998 from the Upper Hudson Library System

FROM CORNBREAD TO KUGEL TO KUCHEN TO KWANZAA
A MULTICULTURAL CELEBRATION

By Dorothy Holt

For five hours on a December Saturday in 1994, a steady stream of people deferred holiday shopping and other entertainment to participate in "From Cornbread to Kugel to Kuchen to Kwanzaa: A Multicultural Celebration" at the Guilderland Public Library.

Guilderland, sometimes described as a "wooded suburb," is west of Albany, the state capital. Its name is a corruption of Gelderland, a Dutch province in the Netherlands and the architecture hearkens back to the days of the early Dutch and German farmers. Walter Dumaux Edmonds depicts Guilderland in the children's novel, *The Matchlock Gun*. The town enjoys a rich cultural and historical heritage and celebrates its tercentennial in 2003.

The library was begun by the Westbrook Women's Club Library Committee with 900 books and five dollars for a start-up fund in a door-to-door campaign. In 1957, the Guilderland Free Library became a reality and operated with an all-volunteer staff for the next six years. In 1988 a resolution was presented to the voters authorizing the establishment of a school district public library to be governed by an elected Board of Trustees. Once the chartered status of the library was changed, progress moved rapidly. School district residents approved a 4.5 million dollar proposal for construction of a 27,650 square foot library in 1990. After being housed in a laundry building, a shopping center, and an office building, the library ultimately settled in its current state-of-the-art space in 1992. The library's building is a programmer's dream. It is beautiful, spacious, accessible and very inviting to our growing and increasingly diverse community of over 30,000 residents.

Flyer for "From Cornbread to Kugel to Kuchen to Kwanzaa"
Guilderland P. L., December 1994

The "Cornbread..." program was a response to our changing community. The time was ripe for a multicultural program! Sensing the limitations of a Christmas or Hanukkah program, I suggested a New Year celebration incorporating traditions of the ethnic groups in the community. We received sustained support from the library staff, who quickly saw the potential of the idea. Joan Barron, a librarian in Youth Services and Reference, had extensive contacts within the community and was able to identify established celebrations. Several Youth Services librarians played an active role – Stephanie Kraus prepared lively graphics and posters, Leslie Saperstone tirelessly formatted recipes and information on New Year celebrations, Joy Lustig arranged Hanukkah games, and

I had significant contacts from various communities from prior work in New York State agencies.

Through our library newsletter I contacted ethnic restaurants for food donations and invited community members to cook. For simplicity, we provided only finger food—toothpicks and napkins, no plates. To locate food and entertainment for the program, I made over one hundred phone calls. Finding participants and summoning the courage to contact them was easier with the support and enthusiasm of so many others: my colleague Joan Barron; Richard Horan, ESL Coordinator at the International Center of the Capital Region, Inc., an organization which assists the foreign-born in the Capital Region; Adi Irani of the Sitar Restaurant, who not only donated food but referred us to the Hindu Temple's cultural organization which sponsored the Indian dancers; Ruby Beaulieu, then Native American Chair of "Keepers of the Circle," and Ms. Andy Spence, Executive Director of Old Songs, Inc. and consultant on folk, traditional, Celtic and world music. Old Songs, Inc. publishes a resource directory for music referrals in the Capital Region. Also, arrangements were made to present a traveling exhibition on the Albany immigrant experience from the Albany Institute of History and Art curated by Wesley Balla.

Six weeks ahead we contacted the Albany League of Arts calendar, to assure as few conflicts with other events as possible. Reporters found the title and concept intriguing. We received publicity in the entertainment listings and in news and feature articles. Flyers were sent home with Guilderland's schoolchildren. Churches, synagogues, temples and ethnic community centers were invited; flyers were posted in restaurants and shops.

On the day of the program, when we opened the doors to our small meeting room, guests found a 25-foot-long table loaded with over twenty-five different ethnic foods. We assembled this cornucopia with a combination of gifts, monetary donations, and volunteer cookery. The core of the feast was generous contributions from three local area restaurants. The Friends of the Library gave us $187 to purchase unique food items from small ethnic restaurants, which were unable to make a donation. Library volunteers Claire Nolan, Marcia Luther, Elizabeth Worden and John Rowen picked up the food and worked tirelessly in the kitchen.

Some participants baked assorted dishes, such as Palestinian and Greek baklava. Those who donated their cooking were rewarded with large signs announcing their contribution. The samples included Indian pakora, nan and vegetable samosa; Palestinian and Greek hummus, pita and babaganoush; Native American cornbread; Caribbean meat patties; French 'Port Salut' cheese; Hungarian salami; Mexican chimichanga; Italian cannoli; Jewish challah, Chinese sweet and sour pork; Vietnamese steamed bun cake and Saigon sandwich; Irish soda bread; German kuchen and Dutch chocolates. We "sandwiched" the food-tasting portion of our program between the morning program of cultural displays, storytelling, and Tae Kwon Do exhibitions and the afternoon musical and dancing entertainment.

Our large meeting room, which seats 150 people, was transformed into a "global marketplace," as one reporter termed it. Together with the program participants, we decorated the room with fine fabrics, artwork, and artifacts from different countries. Here, patrons could have their fortunes told; peruse Chinese silks, porcelain and artwork; examine the Latin American flags, piñata and embroidered dresses; observe Palestinian clothing; consider the significance of the Jewish Hanukkah setting; and marvel at huge Nigerian baskets, jewelry, fabric and dresses. Also on display were Armenian artifacts; Korean fabric and music; Native American beadwork and Chinese brush painting.

Against the exquisite array of exhibits, Barbara Palumbo, storyteller with "Four Stories High," told folktales from around the world to a captive audience of adults and children. John Bye, and students from Bye's Tae Kwon Do studio, demonstrated their skills.

This colorful "Marketplace" became our setting for the afternoon's entertainment. The excellent entertainers included:

- a group of girl dancers from India, whose spokesperson explained the significance of their dance

- Bobba Culpa, a twelve-piece Macedonian and Bulgarian band, dressed in native garb, that succeeded in getting adults and children alike to dance, including the "Miserlou". Before our eyes, Macedonia and Greece were reunited for forty minutes!

- Isaac Rabovskiy, a balalaika player and Yakov Yerusalimskiy, an exuberant singer of Russian ballads as well as a vigorous, robust dancer, left hearts beating madly, begging for more.

- Dutch Horlepiep dancers returned our audience to Guilderland's Dutch roots with their colorful costumes, wooden shoes, and chocolate treats for the children in the spirit of St. Nicholas.

We were able to offer a small honorarium of fifty dollars to most performers; others generously donated their talents. We sent thank you letters with newspaper clippings to all the participants. Our program not only created a forum for discussion of different customs and an opportunity for people proud of their heritage to participate, but it was a step toward tolerance, understanding and affection for one's neighbors.

Participants had this to say:

— Ruby Beaulieu, Chair of Keepers of the Circle: "Thank you for inviting us to participate in the recent multicultural event at the library. I also want you to know how much we enjoyed being a part of it. We know how much time, effort and skill are involved in putting together such a successful program."

— Anneke Bull, spokesperson for the Horlepiep Dancers: "My compliments for a well-organized day. In all my years of this type of event, I can assure you the library deserves an A++!"

This program won an award for Outstanding Program of the Year for 1994 from the Upper Hudson Library System.

HUNTINGTON

CELEBRATE BLACK POETRY DAY!

By Stanley A. Ransom

In 1965, while Director of the Huntington Public Library, on Long Island's North Shore, I kept finding references to one Jupiter Hammon, an eighteenth century Black slave poet belonging to Henry Lloyd, who resided on Lloyd's Neck, a community just to the north of Huntington Village. Seeking to learn more about this man, I researched his writings in local libraries, the Long Island Historical Society, the New–York Historical Society, and the Connecticut Historical Society. Out of this came my book, *America's First Negro Poet; the Complete Works of Jupiter Hammon of Long Island*, published in May, 1970, by Kennikat Press of Port Washington. These were the complete existing writings of Jupiter Hammon and also a compilation of earlier writings about him. The term "Negro" was used in the title instead of "Black" after consultation with Black leaders in the community, who informed me that "Black" was a pejorative term at that time.

The book received a Certificate of Commendation by the American Association for State and Local History in 1972. All copies soon sold out and Associated Faculty Press, a division of Kraus Reprint, issued a second edition, now out of print, in 1983. The book uncovered the date of Hammon's birth, October 17, 1711, and noted that Hammon's first poem, entitled "An Evening Thought," was dated December 25, 1760, some ten years prior to poems composed by another Black poet, Phyllis Wheatley. Hammon, in fact, was not only aware of her verse, but he composed a poem addressed to her in 1778. Some of Hammon's poetry, mostly religious, was composed in Hartford, Connecticut, where Hammon's patriot master had fled during the Revolutionary War. Upon the demise of his master, Hammon became the property of John Lloyd, a Loyalist, and returned again to Lloyd's Neck in Huntington, then occupied by British troops. Hammon was well read, and his friends assisted in the publication of his poems. By a remarkable coincidence, my seventh great-grandfather, Reverend Solomon Stoddard of Northampton, Massachusetts, and first Librarian of Harvard College, was the author of one of the works quoted by Jupiter Hammon in "An Evening's Improvement," a prose sermon published in 1783.

I proposed the establishment of Black Poetry Day annually on October 17th with this purpose: "To recognize the contribution of Black poets to American life and culture and to honor Jupiter Hammon, first Black in America to publish his own verse." As Nikki Giovanni has said, "Poetry is part of the strong oral tradition of Black people." Julius Lester also said, "Poetry is the major expression of Black experience." In Huntington there was a growing concern for the status and condition of Black members of the community, and I helped work to support the Huntington Freedom Center, a source of information, advocacy and assistance to the Black community. As "The Connecticut Peddler," my folksinging alter ego, I performed at benefits for the Freedom Center.

At the Huntington Public Library a Black Poetry Day Committee was formed, chaired by reference librarian Arlene Straughn, and including members of the staff. The six public libraries of Huntington Township at Cold Spring Harbor, Huntington, Northport, Commack, Half Hollow Hills and South Huntington got together to promote the first celebration of Black Poetry Week, October 11–17, 1970. Huntington Supervisor Jerome Ambro issued the first proclamation proclaiming the day of October 17th as Black Poetry Day and asking "all citizens to recognize the need for and the unique contribution of the Black poets in our society." The Performing Arts Foundation of Huntington presented "Readings from the Black Poets" on Friday, October 16th at

the Huntington Public Library. The observance of Black Poetry
Day continued for the next three or four years, with the Long Is-
land-based poet June Jordan as the guest speaker on Sunday, October 17th, 1971, and with funding from Poets and Writers, Inc.,
who are funded by the New York State Council on the Arts.
Jerome Ambro continued to issue yearly proclamations for Black
Poetry Day in Huntington. I received permission in 1971 to use
and publish the following poem by Alicia Loy Johnson, entitled
"Black Poetry Day":

> I am waiting for
> a day when thousands
> will gather before
> shops and stores.
>
> I am waiting for
> a day when thousands
> of BLACKS will listen
> to the words of BLACK POETS
> I am waiting for
> a Black Poetry Day.

In 1974, I became the Director of the Clinton–Essex–Franklin
Library System, in Plattsburgh, New York, and with a new job
could not devote the time to promotion of Black Poetry Day. I did
lecture on several occasions on Long Island, in the North Country,
and for the Ethnic Services Round Table of the New York Library
Association on Jupiter Hammon and his poetry and urged the ob-
servance of Black Poetry Day. I then formed another Black Poetry
Day Committee, under my Chairmanship, and we applied to the
New York State Council on the Arts for annual funding. The
Committee was enlarged to include community and Black leaders
in the Plattsburgh area. As it happened, my marriage to librarian
Christina R. Darden in 1980 joined me with a bi-racial family, and

our daughter, Shani Aisha Darden, is now a model in Los Angeles, giving me an additional reason to promote this special day.

The C-E-F Library System produced a 17-page selected bibliography on "Black American Poetry," a Black Poetry Day bookmark, a sample Proclamation, and a flyer describing Jupiter Hammon and his contribution. Information was sent to *Chase's Calendar of Events* and this announcement brought requests for information and copies of materials from many libraries and military establishments throughout the country and from military installations in Germany.

Our bibliography was adopted by the NAACP in Massachusetts, and in several communities was used by local schools in celebration of Black History Month and for appreciation of Black culture. We sent materials to the San Diego school system and many other schools. Funding was obtained to continue the promotion from the New York State Council on the Arts, from Plattsburgh Air Force Base, and from Plattsburgh State University College (especially the Multicultural Affairs Committee), and from community groups, such as the Dr. Martin Luther King, Jr. Commission of Plattsburgh. We also involved Akeba and El Pueblo, the college's Black and Hispanic student organizations.

During the 1980's we also commissioned several Black Poetry Day posters, done by SUNY faculty member Rick Salzman, which were sent to all our twenty-nine member public libraries and to any interested parties. The Strathmore Paper Company awarded prizes for these outstanding posters.

The celebration of Black Poetry Day under my direction continued until my retirement in November 1991. After this the Chairmanship went to Janet Saunders, Director of the Affirmative Action Program for SUNY Plattsburgh and to Professor Alexis Levitin, Professor of English and Poetry at the college and to Professor of Languages Thomas Braga. Later the chairmanship went to Marlene Fields, Director of the Educational Opportunity Program at SUNY Plattsburgh. The committee included staff members of the C-E-F Library System, college librarians, local artists and community members. I continued to be an active member of the committee.

The celebration of Black Poetry Day was proclaimed by our city mayors, Carlton Rennell and Clyde Rabideau, and in some years by Governor Mario Cuomo. Many New York State public and school libraries joined in the celebration. The Proclamation samples we sent were used in many communities.

Our speakers were the best we could find, and they were all excellent. We met in the College auditorium, which was accessible to the handicapped. We met at 7:30 in the evening, which was best for those traveling some distance. We always obtained a supply of the speaker's books at a discount which we then sold for somewhat less than retail. We wanted people to have the books, rather than using the sales to make money. Purchasers were delighted to have the speaker inscribe them.

Our programs were attended by schoolchildren, college students, Air Base personnel, community families, the Black community, community and college leaders, and interested persons from fifty miles away. Robin Caudell, a local poet and Black news reporter, gave us excellent coverage in the local *Press-Republican* newspaper.

Our audience averaged about 150 persons, with a few exceptions. In 1985 Gwendolyn Brooks drew an audience of 225 people. She also consented to visit our state correctional facility in Dannemora, where she entranced 100 inmates, many of them trying to write poetry. In 1992, we had engaged Derek Walcott to speak. The announcement of his Nobel Prize for Literature award came the week before he was to speak, and we held our breath that this entry into clamorous fame would not disturb his schedule. He arrived with great local fanfare and read poetry to more than 600 students and community members, who listened in rapt attention. It is a great day when Black poetry can attract 600 listeners.

Poster (18"x24") designed by Rick Salzman for 1985 Black Poetry Day, which was distributed to all system libraries and the Plattburgh community

Here is the list of guest speakers since Black Poetry Day was established:

- 1970: Performing Arts Foundation of Huntington: Selected Readings
- 1971: June Jordan
- 1972-1974 (local readings)
- 1984: June Jordan (First Plattsburgh Observance)
- 1985: Gwendolyn Brooks; Linda Cousins at Saranac Lake Free Library
- 1986: Sam Cornish
- 1987: Nikki Giovanni
- 1988: Amiri Baraka and Blue Ark jazz players
- 1989: Bernard Finney
- 1990: Quincy Troupe

- 1991: Lucille Clifton
- 1992: Derek Walcott, 1992 Nobel Prize for Literature
- 1993: Ntozake Shange
- 1994: Michael Harper, Poet Laureate of Rhode Island, who also toured the several local Underground Railroad sites;
- 1995: Jusef Koumanyaka, Pulitzer Prize for Poetry
- 1996: Jackie Warren-Moore
- 1997: Allison Joseph
- 1998: Cornelius Eady
- 1999: Kevin Young

The lesson we learned was that Black Poetry Day is a wonderful way to link all parts of the community. There is a great need for programs that show the positive side of Black life. There is a need for children to be exposed to successful and creative role models. There is an opportunity for libraries to make a difference in their communities through the medium of programs of poetry, especially Black poetry. We hope that Black Poetry Day will be the vehicle for enabling libraries to perform a valuable service to their community residents. Our message: Celebrate Black Poetry Day!

LAFAYETTE

PUTTING A FACE ON IT
PUBLIC LIBRARY OUTREACH TO DIVERSE POPULATIONS

By Cara Jane Burton

"Hey, I know you! You're the library lady!" yells out a pre-schooler. It's music to my ears when this child recognizes me and thinks of the library. It means we have accomplished our outreach goal. The child has one of the building blocks for learning about the world of reading. Familiarity with the librarian will hopefully stir interest in the library.

When I interviewed as Director of the LaFayette Public Library in 1998, the Board of Trustees expressed a strong interest in developing the Native American area in the collection. Although the library as a municipal library is chartered to serve the Town of LaFayette, the Trustees feel responsible to serve the town's neighboring Onondaga Nation. The LaFayette School District includes the Onondaga Nation and the Onondaga teens attend the central high school. The Onondaga Nation does not have a public library.

Acquiring books was easy, as there are many good Native American writers, Native American folktales, and political science books, not to mention several series on tribes and history. But what good were these books if no one checked them out, except to say that we were sensitive to these issues? Besides making the public library attractive to the Onondagas with our collection, we decided to develop an outreach program to increase awareness of the library and the comfort level for using it.

Residents of the Onondaga Nation do not frequently use LaFayette Public Library. The reasons are varied. Geography and transportation are the obvious obstruction as an Interstate runs between the library and the Nation with no nearby crossover bridges. A city library is closer for most Onondagas. In designing any programs, we knew we would be providing outreach to another nation and it was important to respect their borders and concern for privacy. Tensions exist with their Anglo neighbors because of cultural differences and prejudice.

A patron registration count is unavailable because the county library system does not recognize the Onondagas, or their Nation, in the patron information codes. From our own observation and that of the city library close to the Nation, Onondagas do not frequently use the public libraries. The Onondaga Nation has an excellent library in a new elementary school that is administered by the LaFayette School District, but it is geared towards grades K through 6 and opens only during school hours.

Target groups were determined by the availability of access to them. Whenever opportunity knocked, we've grabbed it, but as I look back, outreach has mainly been directed toward children because of the school district connection. What little I knew of the Onondagas advised me to ease into their programs. An "in your face" approach would definitely turn people off. Attention to sensitivities about respect for animals, hunters, and indigenous peoples would have to apply to book selection, too. Attendance at Nation cultural events and pow-wows offered a fun way to become more aware of the Onondaga's culture.

Many of the children are served by storyhours at the LaFayette Headstart where attendance is 50 percent Native American. The little boy mentioned earlier heard me read stories at the Headstart School every other week. Reaching out to these preschoolers provides a chance to talk about the public library and gives them a familiar face to see when they come to visit.

A cooperative of area social services called "Connections for Families and Children in Southern Onondaga" provides an excellent resource for networking with the community. Every other month, representatives of area educational, clinical and social services meet to discuss health and literacy issues in the southern part of the county and the Onondaga Nation. These meetings provide a forum to announce new programs and services, identify new information needs in the community, and meet key community leaders. The library, being a public access facility with a variety of open hours, also acts as a clearinghouse for the cooperative. Because of the networking, a connection was made with a social worker at the Onondaga Nation Clinic.

This family advocate organizes playgroups on the Nation for toddlers and preschoolers. Playgroups help warm up the kids for socializing at Headstart and gives the mothers a chance to socialize and talk with the social worker. She invites me to read to the kids occasionally and pass out library literature to the mothers. I recognize these mothers at school and cultural events.

School age children participate in after school and summer school programs. Booktalks, special storytelling, career days, and table displays at school fairs all provide opportunities to share information and provide a familiar face. We also visit schools to register students for library cards. In these ways, we become familiar with the students and they with us.

Mini-libraries have been a way to include Onondaga Nation children in the summer reading program without the constraints of transportation, library registration, rules, fines, and deadlines. A decorated box of books is placed in the health clinic along with the summer reading program forms to record books, bookmarks, and program announcements. It is kind of a do-it-yourself reading program. Kids can borrow the books without any registration or due dates. A label on the chapter and picture books says, "I am a library book. Read Me! Then share me with a friend or return me here so I can be read again!" The used books are obtained from donations or library discards. Two other mini-libraries and reading program materials were provided to summer school programs at the Nation school.

Outreach services are just beginning at LaFayette Public Library, so measurement of success is only available by observation and intuition at this point. Being a small community, we can follow the preschoolers seen during storyhours through school and observe their attendance at the library. This library doesn't agree with the "if you build it, they will come" philosophy, because these days, the library takes on more roles than that of a book warehouse. Traditional modes of communication such as flyers, newspaper articles, calendars of events, and Web sites are not always the most effective in reaching special populations. By physically going out into the community, the library involves itself in the education of area children. They are learning that the library is people too, because we are "putting a face" on it.

NEW ROCHELLE

THIS IS OUR HOME
ÉSTE ES NUESTRO HOGAR
THE ANTONIO VALENCIA LOCAL HISTORY COLLECTION
AT THE NEW ROCHELLE PUBLIC LIBRARY

BY ROBIN OSBORNE

The New York State Archives, Documentary Heritage Services awarded the Westchester Library System two grants (1999–2001) for a program to identify, collect, and preserve records that document the post-war migration and settlement of diverse ethnic populations in the cities, towns, and villages of Westchester County. The underlying premises of the program model are: (1) that public libraries should actively seek information and resources about unique populations vital to the social and historical narrative of the larger community, and (2) that libraries should actively collect and organize those resources.

The prototype for the program is based at the New Rochelle Public Library, and seeks to identify and survey records of significant organizations and leaders of that city's Mexican community. The story begins with Antonio Valencia, who arrived in 1954, alone and speaking not a word of English, to serve as a live-in housekeeper for George Vergara, a former mayor of New Rochelle, and his wife Allys. In 1955, Valencia arranged for three others from his hometown of Quitupán to move to his new city. He continued correspondence with friends and family in Quitupán, and worked with local businesses and families to find employment and homes for them in New Rochelle. More and more people from Quitupán and neighboring villages found their way to *El Dorado* (the name of a waterfront country club in New Rochelle). Valencia became a conduit for Mexican immigrants seeking assistance in immigration matters, education, health care, and other services. According to the 1990 census, approximately 11 percent of the residents of New Rochelle are Hispanic, mostly of Mexican origin. Many believe that those of Mexican descent now account for 15 to 20 percent of the population, the majority of whom originated from Mr. Valencia's region of Mexico. There are dozens of Mexican businesses and cultural groups in the city, and many doctors, lawyers, and accountants in the community. Mr. Valencia is recognized as the patriarch of the Mexican community in New Rochelle, and has been honored by the Consul General of Mexico in the New York region, and by the governor of his home state, Jalisco.

Project activities began with the formation of an advisory board, which currently includes members of the Mexican community, library staff at the Westchester Library System and New Rochelle Public Library, and a bilingual project archivist. The board convened an initial meeting with Mr. Valencia in November 1999 to get an idea of the general history of the relocation and to identify contacts and families who could provide vital information.

A draft survey was then written to learn more about the community. The survey included a query as to the types of documents, photos and other memorabilia that individuals kept and would be willing to share with the project. A limited distribution of the survey received an enthusiastic response. One woman immediately donated two letters and several photos of her home in Mexico. The survey was later revised and translated into Spanish (see Appendices 1 and 2).

Individuals have provided many documents and other items of interest to the project. Project staff have also sought records of institutions such as local churches, school districts, and city offices, as well as cultural organizations within the Mexican community. Records of membership and finances, as well as calendars of meetings and events, will be valuable additions to the collection.

In one instance, an interview was conducted with the Director of the Department for Community Relations of the Mexican Consulate in New York City, who offered access to the files of that organization. These files include photos, letters, and other documents relating to Mr. Valencia and the community in New Rochelle.

The Antonio Valencia Local History Collection was established in the summer of 2000. The first major donation came from Mr. Valencia's personal collection, and included letters, photographs, passports, newspaper clippings, and other documents. Mr. Valencia's material reflects his own accomplishments in support and promotion of smooth transition for Mexican immigrants into this community, as well as the impact of financial aid and other support sent back to his village in Mexico. Letters and newspaper articles in this collection illustrate Valencia's efforts in finding employment for newcomers, as well as financing the construction of a school and employment of teachers in Mexico. Photographs were also donated by the Mexican Consulate that depict the honors bestowed on Mr. Valencia in connection with his support of religious and other cultural organizations.

As of this writing, twenty-four surveys have been completed. Our goal is to compile at least fifty more. We have recently partnered with instructors at the New Americans Resource Center at the New Rochelle Public Library (a project funded by the U.S. Department of Education to provide English literacy and civics education for immigrants in the community), who are incorporating completion of the survey in their lesson plans. Once these surveys are completed and compiled, the Project Archivist will work with respondents about accessing records — either through donation to the library or by temporary loan to allow photocopying or digital scanning of items. The library can then reproduce individual records on acid-free paper to house in its facility, for easy access by local residents and students of all ages. Originals can be transferred to the Westchester County Historical Society for optimum storage.

The project Advisory Committee encourages active participation from both the Mexican community and other residents of New Rochelle. On June 4, 2000, a day of cultural celebration was held in Antonio Valencia's name to launch this project. Samples of donated material, promotional and informational leaflets, in both Spanish and English, were displayed and handed out. More than 200 attended this event, which featured performances by traditional music and dance groups, as well as the presentation of a Proclamation from the City of New Rochelle in Mr. Valencia's honor. The library will create the position of Guest Curator—a member of the Mexican community—to work with library staff on an ongoing basis to support the expansion and use of the collection at the New Rochelle Public Library.

Another way that the library can engage with members of the community is to initiate the process of recording oral histories as a means to provide a rich and complex insight into social and cultural life. This process will be facilitated by Professor Roger Panetta of Marymount College, who will prepare and counsel his students, many of whom are bilingual, to conduct interviews with members of the Mexican community—both early settlers and newcomers. The tapes and transcripts of the interviews will be donated to the Antonio Valencia collection.

The enthusiasm and success of the project to date has enabled staff to think about how other libraries can modify or replicate the New Rochelle model, and how the model can be used to promote understanding and appreciation for the diverse cultural communities that now inhabit the county. Future plans for the collection include the development of a CD-ROM product and a Web site hosted by the New Rochelle Public Library. These will display digital images of the documents, photos, and other ephemera collected, with the addition of spoken and written narrative to provide a historical and cultural framework for the general user. These products may then be used in schools, libraries, and homes to demonstrate a unique history of one immigrant community, as well as to highlight issues that cross cultural and linguistic boundaries to reflect a common history in Westchester. The project offers an entry into the social history of a vital part of the New Rochelle landscape, accessible through primary and secondary sources. It will serve as a model by which other Westchester libraries and communities can chronicle the experiences of the rich and varied patchwork of cultures that immigrated to the county in the past fifty years.

Appendix 1

The New Rochelle Public Library and the Westchester Library System are seeking assistance from the Mexican community of New Rochelle for a project to document the settlement of this community over the past fifty years. Many believe that the Mexican community now accounts for 15–20 percent of the population. There are dozens of businesses and cultural groups in the city, and many have achieved great success as they made their lives in the United States. We would like to expand the library's local history collection to include the story of the migration and settlement of Mexican residents in New Rochelle. In order to tell this story and collect the necessary materials, we need to interview people, and identify letters, photos, and other documents that chronicle this journey. These pieces would then be organized and preserved as part of the library's collection, and available to all residents, adults and children, as evidence of the Mexican community and its contributions to the city of New Rochelle.

Please answer the questions below. We would appreciate suggestions of other ideas by which we can document the activities of this community. If you have any questions or concerns, please contact Robin Osborne at the Westchester Library System at (914) 674-3600, ext. 237.

Thank you for your support of this project.

SURVEY QUESTIONS

1. Names of respondent
   Address
   Phone number
2. Why and when did you and/or your family come to New Rochelle?
3. Did you know anyone in New Rochelle before arriving? (please write the name of that person)
4. Who was the first to arrive? (please write full name)
1. In sequence, who were the family members that followed (please write full names)?
2. What village/state are you from?
3. How many years of school did you attend in Mexico?
4. Did you learn to read and/or speak English before your arrival?
5. Where in New Rochelle did you first live?
6. What type of work did you do in Mexico?
7. How did you get your first job in New Rochelle? What kind of job was it?
8. Do you remember what you brought with you from Mexico when you moved here (e.g., photos, clothing, cooking utensils, etc.)?
9. Please give the names of your children who were born in New Rochelle and their dates of birth.
10. What schools did they attend?
11. What church/house of worship did you attend when you came to New Rochelle?

12. What other organizations did you join (e.g., El Club Cultural, religious societies, etc.)?
13. Do you visit_____
    telephone_____write_____with family in Mexico? How frequently?
14. Are other members of your family or community planning to move to New Rochelle in the future?
15. Do you have any of the following that we could see:
    Photos
    Letters/correspondence
    Birth/death certificates
    Immigration/naturalization papers
    Family videos
    Recipes
    Passports
    Travel tickets
    Postcards
    Letters
    Musical recordings
    Other

Appendix 2

La Biblioteca Pública de New Rochelle y el Sistema de Bibliotecas Públicas del Condado de Westchester solicitan la ayuda de la comunidad mexicana de New Rochelle para llevar a cabo un proyecto con el fin de documentar el establecimiento de esta comunidad en los últimos cincuenta años. Muchos piensan que la comunidad mexicana constituye el 15–20% del total de la población. Hay docenas de negocios y grupos culturales en la ciudad, y muchos han alcanzado el éxito al forjar sus vidas en los Estados Unidos. Nos gustaría expandir la colección de historia local de la biblioteca incluyendo la historia de la migración y establecimiento de los residentes mexicanos en New Rochelle. Para contar esta historia y reunir los materiales necesarios, tenemos que entrevistar a la gente e identificar cartas, fotos y otros documentos que sirvan como crónica de este viaje. Dichas piezas serán organizadas y preservadas como parte de la colección de la biblioteca que quedará disponible para todos los residentes, niños y adultos, como prueba de la comunidad mexicana y su contribución a la ciudad de New Rochelle.

Por favor, conteste las preguntas que figuran a continuación. Nos gustaría recibir sugerencias y otras ideas que nos ayuden a documentar las actividades de esta comunidad. Si tiene alguna pregunta o preocupación, por favor llame a Robin Osborne del Sistema de Bibliotecas Públicas del Condado de Westchester al (914) 674-3600, interno 237.

Muchas gracias por su apoyo.

PREGUNTAS DE LA ENCUESTA

1. Nombre de la persona encuestada
   Dirección
   Número de teléfono
2. ¿Cuándo y por qué usted y /o los miembros de su familia vinieron a New Rochelle?
3. ¿Conocía a alguien en New Rochelle antes de llegar? (Por favor escriba el nombre de esta persona)
4. ¿Quién fue el primero en llegar? (Por favor escriba el nombre completo)
5. En orden de llegada, ¿quiénes fueron los miembros de la familia que vinieron después? (Por favor escriba los nombres completos)
6. ¿De qué villa / estado es usted?
7. ¿Cuántos años de escuela cursó en México?
8. ¿Aprendió a leer y / o escribir inglés antes de su llegada?
9. ¿En que parte de New Rochelle vivió primero?

10. ¿Qué tipo de trabajo tenía en México?
11. ¿Cómo obtuvo el primer trabajo en New Rochelle? ¿Qué tipo de trabajo era?
12. ¿Recuerda qué cosas trajó de México cuando se mudó aquí (Por ejemplo: fotos, ropa, utensilios de cocina, etc.)?
13. Por favor escriba los nombres de sus hijos nacidos en New Rochelle y la fecha de nacimiento.
14. ¿A qué escuelas concurrieron?
15. ¿A qué iglesia concurría cuando llegó a New Rochelle?
16. ¿De qué otras organizaciones se hizo miembro? (Por ejemplo: El Club Cultural, sociedades religiosas, etc.)
17. ¿Visita ___, llama por teléfono ___, o le escribe ___ a su familia en México? ¿Qué tan a menudo?
18. ¿Otros miembros de su familia o comunidad están planeando mudarse a New Rochelle en el futuro?
19. ¿Tiene algunos de los siguientes artículos que nos pueda mostrar?

Fotografías
Cartas / Correspondencia
Certificados de Nacimiento / Defunción
Papeles de inmigración y naturalización
Videos familiares
Recetas
Pasaportes
Pasajes
Postales
Cartas
Grabaciones musicales
Otros

NEW YORK CITY

ACCENTS FROM THE BIG APPLE

A BRIEF HISTORY OF SERVICES
TO SPEAKERS OF LANGUAGES OTHER THAN ENGLISH
AT THE DONNELL WORLD LANGUAGES COLLECTION
THE NEW YORK PUBLIC LIBRARY

By Bosiljka Stevanovic

Since its founding, New York City and its area have attracted immigrants from throughout the world. Waves of European immigration poured into the city seeking a better life and a free land, and eighteen languages were already spoken in the tiny Dutch colony at the time when Peter Stuyvesant (1592–1672) was its governor. In time, the concentration of people and cultures transformed New York from a small colony to a teeming metropolis and, to this day, it has not ceased to be the preferred port of entry for immigrants.

In the last few decades New York City has seen new waves of immigration. The new immigrants, be they from Russia, Eastern Europe, Africa, Asia, Southeast Asia, India, the Middle East, South America, or the Caribbean Islands, essentially come to America for the same reasons as did the previous immigrant groups, namely to make a better life for themselves and their families, or to flee persecution and hardships of one form or another. Now, as in the past, hundreds of thousands of new immigrants choose to settle in New York and its surrounding areas, and in the process the character of certain neighborhoods often changes as the groups replace one another.

The New York Public Library has a well-documented history of services to the numerous populations of speakers of other languages going back to the end of the nineteenth century. This type of service seems to have evolved spontaneously in response to the needs of the neighborhoods' multi-ethnic and multilingual populations. The records, going back to the 1880's, show a number of branches offering services to specific groups. Thus, branches such as Aguilar, Chatham Square, Ottendorfer, Tompkins Square, 115th Street, Seward Park, and Webster have been both front-runners, as well as long-distance runners, in serving neighborhoods from the Lower East Side to the Upper West Side with Italian, German, Hungarian, Polish, Chinese, Hebrew, Yiddish, Czech and Spanish-speaking populations then, and new ones at present, such as Arabic, Indian, Russian, Eastern European, Vietnamese, and more.

Over the years, the original character of the neighborhoods served by the above-mentioned branches changed. The earlier populations either moved away or died out, and collections, once the source of branch and neighborhood pride, became neglected and obsolete. At that point it was felt that a consolidation of such collections in one central place would be a more desirable solution. In December 1955, when the New York Public Library opened a new building, the Donnell Library Center at 20 West 53rd Street in Manhattan, many of those diverse and dispersed collections were transferred to this new home and consolidated into one large collection of books in languages other than English. It was called the Foreign Language Library and it opened with approximately 19,000 volumes in nineteen languages. From the first annual report in August of 1956 by the then Supervising Librarian, Earle M. Gladden, we read that, by the time of the report, there were additions to the stock (4,000 books) as well as additions of languages. The major collections were Russian (10,000 volumes), French (3,000), German (2,500), Italian (1,700), Hungarian (1,200), Yiddish (1,000), Danish/Norwegian/Swedish (600), Spanish (500, originally 99), Modern Greek (400) and Finnish (400). Medium-sized collections were Polish (300 volumes), Hebrew (250), Chinese (200), Japanese (200), Armenian (170), Czech (160), Portuguese (50), Dutch (135) and Lithuanian (77). Smaller and token collections included: Afrikaans, Esperanto, English (bilingual dictionaries), Flemish, Romanian (according to the report, "the most asked for language...”), Yugoslav (Serbian, Croatian, Slovenian and Macedonian), Catalan, Gaelic, Korean, Malayan and Persian.

The circulation figures for the first 7 1/2 months showed an awesome figure of 61,000 books, with the circulation of Russian books accounting for more than one-half of the entire circulation. Russian circulation was followed, in order, by that of French, German, Hungarian, Italian and Spanish. The last circulated 152 books while having 99 books in its collection! The only language that did not circulate was Lithuanian, but, according to the report, it picked up later.

The question then was, as it is now, what other languages were needed to serve such a diverse population as that of New York City. A notebook was provided for readers' suggestions and the requests received indicated demands for Arabic, Romanian, Persian, Gaelic, Japanese, Serbian, Bulgarian, Ukrainian, Croatian, Chinese, Afrikaans, Dutch, Turkish, Swahili, Urdu, Catalan, Vietnamese, Hindi and Estonian. Since books in a number of these languages were already available, the argument was made to develop Arabic, Hindi and Swahili collections, which represented the Near East, the Indian subcontinent, and Africa. It was equally important to “have a fair representation of the world's chief languages” as well as to make a case for inclusion and diversity. There were no requests entered in the notebook for Russian, Spanish or French! Today, Spanish (32,720), Russian (24,311), Chinese (15,046), and French (13,744) constitute the largest collections, while Turkish and Swahili are rarely asked for, and yet rarer are the requests for Catalan and Gaelic.

Following Mr. Gladden's vision of growth and improvements for the Foreign Language Library, the unit developed substantially in the intervening forty-five years. Having succeeded Mr. Gladden as the Supervising Librarian of the unit in 1978, I can testify to the many changes and developments since then. Among other things, in 1994 the name was changed to the World Languages Collection to better convey the idea of all-encompassing diversity of the population of New York and its surrounding areas. From a collection of 19,000 books in nineteen languages it has grown to about 163,000 items (books, paperbacks, magazines and videos), in about eighty languages. Not only has it grown in size but also in its impact on the lives of many people, who are a long way from home and who are happy to find our library to be "a home away from home." Echoing Mr. Gladden's words, "not a day goes by, but that we are complimented." We, too, can boast of often hearing surprise, delight and gratitude expressed by readers who, discovering us for the first time, find out that our library has books, periodicals and videos in their language. This is also a place where the impact of any political change in the world is felt almost immediately. The newly-arrived immigrants lose no time in finding their way to our library and asking for books in their own language.

Like the changing neighborhoods, the World Languages Collection keeps changing with the times. They keep experiencing the cycle of "life, death, and rebirth," most often following the political whims of the day as illustrated by the following few examples. In the late 1940s a great influx of immigrants, mostly World War II refugees from Europe, created a large demand for books in German and Yiddish, which has subsided in the past few decades as that particular population aged, died out or moved away. Yiddish is particularly affected. There are relatively few speakers of that language now, and publishing activities are practically non-existent. The war in Vietnam and Cambodia brought about the development of the Vietnamese and the Khmer collections. Both languages continue to be very much in demand, though less material is available to buy in Khmer. Also, in the last couple of decades a tremendous influx of Asian immigrants resulted in great expansions of the Korean, Thai and especially the Chinese collections. The ranks of the original Russian readership consisting of émigrés from the Russian Revolution were very much thinned out by the end of the sixties and the collection exhibited signs of demise. The new waves of Russian immigration caused it to be substantially revitalized, and greatly expanded. The newly-arrived immigrants created an unprecedented demand for anything that has ever been, or is being published in the Russian language. The break-up of Yugoslavia led to the separation of Serbo-Croatian into Bosnian, Croatian and Serbian and increased demand for books in Bosnian, Croatian, Serbian, Macedonian and Slovenian. Sending collections of books in a variety of languages on circuit loan to branch libraries is also a part of the services offered to multilingual communities and was put into place a long time ago. At first, a collection named the N.Y.P.L. Central Reserve Collection was maintained for that purpose and it was separate from the Donnell Foreign Language Library. Around the mid-seventies the two collections merged. Supplying books to the branches remains one of our most important activities, and in 1996 we received the Maher–Stern Award "in recognition of exemplary leadership and excellence in community service." In fiscal year 2000 we sent 63,301 books on circuit to the branches.

Also worthy of note is the fact that in 1989 the staff of the World Languages Collection, or the Donnell Foreign Language Library as it was then known, received the Leonard Wertheimer Multilingual Public Library Award in "recognition for their outstanding contributions in enhancing and promoting multilingual public library service." The award was given by the Public Library Association and was based on the bibliographies in languages other than English that have been regularly compiled by the staff and published in the journal *Booklist* since the late 1960s.

Today, in the most diverse era ever, the World Languages Collection at the Donnell Library Center is enjoying popularity and a big demand for its holdings. Our collections are general and popular, emphasizing literature written in the original language. Fiction (classics, contemporary writings and light genre fiction) and non-fiction (covering all areas of the dewey decimal system, when possible) are included, as are periodicals, and feature films on video. Our collections are circulating, and, due to our easily accessible midtown location, many patrons make great use of what we have to offer. Some observable measures of the use of our materials are the number of reserves we see placed (as for example, over 3,000 for books in one Chinese series), and the circulation overall. In fiscal year 2000 the circulation reached one million at the Donnell Library Center, and a great part of that can easily be attributed to the materials circulated from the World Languages Collection. Our readers tend to borrow books by the armful, and we often see them with shopping baskets full of materials to check out.

Among the activities most enjoyed by the staff and patrons alike are our literary and music programs. Over the years, poets, prose writers and musicians from different countries have participated in such programs. Some programs will remain memorable, such as the one organized for the 200th anniversary of A. S. Pushkin (1799–1831), when a group of scholars, literary critics, poets, actors and musicians presented a medley of "Pushkiniana" to an enthralled audience, in spite of an unbearably hot day. Or a symposium discussing the differences in the development of the novel in North America, Latin America and Europe with Norman Mailer, Elena Poniatowska and José Saramago.

We have come a long way from a collection of 19,000 volumes and the days of homemade card catalogs! Not only did the collection grow to be a large one, but we have also made it to the electronic world as well, and thus all our holdings are accessible electronically (http://www.nypl.org) to a larger and wider audience than ever before!

THE CHINESE HERITAGE COLLECTION
AT THE CHATHAM SQUARE REGIONAL BRANCH
THE NEW YORK PUBLIC LIBRARY

By Ronald S. Chan

The Chatham Square Regional Branch is one of the eighty-five neighborhood branches of The New York Public Library system. The branch opened in 1903 at 33 East Broadway, replacing a smaller branch of The New York Free Circulating Library that had served the neighborhood for four years. From the earliest days, Chatham Square Regional Branch has always been an integral part of the community, which has been an area of first settlement for many immigrants. The Chinese have been part of this community since the middle of the nineteenth century and are now overwhelmingly the largest group in the service area. Today, the branch acts as a cultural, civic and information center for a community of avid readers and is one of the busiest libraries in New York City. Recognizing the role and importance of the Chatham Square Regional Branch to the Chinese community, The New York Public Library, in 1983, designated Chatham Square Regional Branch as one of its four Ethnic Heritage Centers. The goal of the Heritage Center is to preserve Chinese culture and heritage and at the same time to provide readers with access to learning and enrichment in books.

Purposes of the Chinese Heritage Collection

The goals of the Chinese Heritage Collection include: acquiring, organizing and providing access to a collection for the general public interested in China, the Chinese, and Chinese American materials; creating a better understanding for, and study of Chinese culture; filling the informational, educational, cultural and recreational needs of the Chinese and Chinese American readership, especially new immigrants, students and reporters doing fact-finding; and satisfying the needs of one of the most up-and-coming ethnic communities, as demonstrated by the continuous influx of new immigrants into the service area.

Function and Scope of the Chinese Heritage Collection

The Chinese Heritage Collection strives: (1) to meet the heavy demand of Chinese readers of all age levels, (2) to serve the many non-Chinese reading Chinese who are looking for their roots, as well as for current writings about China, (3) to serve readers with limited or no English proficiency, (4) to provide native language materials to Chinese immigrants, acting as a cultural crossroads between two cultures, (5) to offer language materials and services to induce readers to take advantage of other library and social services for their children or friends, and (6) to bridge the "digital divide" by providing access to electronic information in English and, using the *Tango* software program, in Chinese.

Administration of the Collection

For the circulating collection of Chinese language materials, Chatham Square Regional Branch buys what the general reader would want (for example, health, computers, business, investment guides, home repairs, job-finding) in Chinese, plus special materials of interest to the Chinese reader. For the English language collection, Chatham Square Regional Branch buys China-related materials such as guidebooks, culture, and history, including materials to meet the particular interest in Chinatown and Chinese Americans.

For the Heritage circulating collection, the branch buys books including popular items such as Chinese herbal medicine, acupuncture, cooking, philosophy, Kung-fu, and Tai-Chi; titles to fill current requests by readers; fiction and non-fiction works, including outstanding novels; materials to fill recreational and entertainment needs, including leisure reading materials; bilingual materials, translations of major Western literature and reference tools; how-to and self-teaching instructional books or guides; materials introducing American culture, history, current events, social and economic life, and travel guides; and books and materials related to the existing collection and its development.

For the Heritage Reference collection, the materials focus on the following areas: Chinese history, literature, philosophy, culture, customs, science and technology; introduction to customs, festivals, arts and crafts, medicine and outstanding biographies; travel and sightseeing guidebooks; historical and general encyclopedic works on China; fact-finding handbooks, data and census materials, informational directories, and atlases.

The overall emphasis is on the essence of Chinese culture, the Chinese in the United States, and New York's Chinatown. The objective of the books in the Chinese in the United States collection is to present information pertaining to the social, cultural, political and economic life experience of the Chinese in the United States or Chinese Americans. This collection has titles such as *Chinese in the United States, Chinese in America, Chinese American Experience, Chinese American Intermarriage, Gangs of New York, New Immigrants in New York, Social and Political Change of New York's Chinatown,* and *Chinatown U.S.A.* This reference section offers a special and unique collection of materials, including reports on Manhattan's Chinatown, and a very popular collection of several local Chinese language newspapers. The Chinatown community files contain clippings from both English and Chinese language newspapers as well as the literature of Chinatown. It has information on local social services and organizations, business and industry (e.g. the restaurant industry, the garment industry, and street vendors), housing, schools, museums, churches and Buddhist temples, and parks and recreation.

Levels of Materials Collected and Subject Areas

Collections include materials for adults, young adults and children. Every attempt is made to provide general interest materials in broad subject areas, covering the complete dewey classification. The Chinese in the United States Collection includes selected research materials (the Chinatown vertical file and the microfilms of the *United Journal* and the *World Journal* are available for research use).

The Greater New York area has the largest population of Asians on the East Coast, and Chatham Square Regional Branch is trying to meet the increased demand for quality service for this burgeoning group of users. Not only is the Asian population on the Lower East Side growing, but in addition, these new residents' strong interest in education and in adapting to the American way of life makes the library an especially important resource within the neighborhood. Often, this is the first opportunity many immigrants have to freely select and read what they like. The residents, who are primarily new immigrants from Mainland China, Vietnam, Thailand, Hong Kong, Cambodia, and Malaysia, thirst for news from their homeland while at the same time voraciously seeking information on assimilating to American life.

COMMUNITY ANALYSIS
FOR THE TWENTY-FIRST CENTURY
THE NEW AMERICANS PROGRAM MODEL

BY FRED J. GITNER AND WAI SZE CHAN

Queens is currently recognized as the most diverse county in the United States, with over 100 languages spoken. With a population of two million, 36 percent of Queens' residents are immigrants, and 44 percent speak a language other than English at home, according to the 1990 census. Since its founding in 1896, Queens Borough Public Library has always been a community-oriented institution committed to serving its diverse and changing population, many of who come from countries without a public library tradition. The New Americans Program, an agency within the Programs and Services Department, provides a wide array of library programs and services geared toward making the library a community center and a place of lifelong learning for newcomers, as well as for more traditional library customers.

From its start in 1977 as a federally-funded project, the New Americans Program had as its goals: "to expand library services to immigrants whose primary language is not English, and to attract newcomers to the library and assist them in adjusting to their new surroundings through acquisition of appropriate materials and creation of special training programs, workshops, and services, while fostering an appreciation for their unique cultural makeup."

A variety of techniques were used to help determine which groups to target, and what programs and services to offer. These included: conducting community studies, surveying branch managers regarding their neighborhoods, and making contacts with police precinct community relations officers and the borough president's office. In addition, the local ethnic press and the telephone directory were examined for possible contacts. Community organizations of many types, including social service, ethnic, schools and churches were contacted. Based on this assessment, groups targeted initially were the Hispanic, Greek and Chinese communities.

Primarily city-funded since the 1980s, programs and services offered include:

- classes in English for Speakers of Other Languages (now part of the library's Adult Learner Program)

- practical Coping Skills workshops such as, "Preparing your Child for High School" in Spanish and "Help Wanted: Interviewing and Resume Writing Skills" in Chinese to help new immigrants adapt to life in America

- Cultural Arts programs to assist immigrants in maintaining their native language and culture and to introduce these cultures to the public at large

- popular collections in languages other than English demonstrating that the library respects their native language, culture and customs

- collections of materials to aid in learning or improving English language skills.

Ongoing community analysis is the key to the success of the New Americans Program. Just as all other service-oriented professions or businesses, we need to know who our customers are and what they really need. This is especially true in a highly culturally-attuned community. A cultural program by a famous Peking Opera performer will attract more than 100 Chinese immigrants who might never bother to visit the library otherwise. A Bengali newspaper could entice immigrant customers to come to the library every day to check out what is going on in their home country, and at the same time they may check out other library materials. On the other hand, having an excellent Russian collection in a Hispanic community will not benefit the residents there. In other words, everything we do is customer-oriented. We use a variety of strategies. We consult with our branch managers who are on the front line and have daily contact with customers and maintain relationships with organizations in their neighborhood. We follow the ethnic media, as well as articles on immigration in the mainstream media. Our staff attends community fairs to make valuable contacts with social service agencies and local performing artists. All of these means give us a better idea of the communities we serve. However, with the large influx of new immigrants coming from all over the world in the early 1990s, we saw the need for tracking them more systematically and precisely. Demographic statistics are available from many government agencies, like the Census Bureau, as well as non-profit organizations. Our ESOL student records are also very useful sample data. All we needed was human intelligence to collect and convert the data into useful input, to aid in planning our services. At the time, in most urban libraries, including the Queens Library, the task of community analysis was shared by librarians who might also be involved in dozens of other duties. However, our Program Head, Adriana A. Tandler, felt strongly about the importance of community analysis and believed that this deserved the full attention of a designated professional staff member. Her vision was supported by the administration and our first Information & Data Analysis Librarian was hired in 1994.

Community analysis has been one of the formal components of the New Americans Program for almost seven years. Although there are a lot of difficulties, there are many rewards as well. The number one difficulty we face is the availability of current, reliable and accurate data. What interests us most is how many people speaking what languages, or from what ethnic backgrounds, live in which neighborhood in Queens. Theoretically, census data is the most authoritative source for this question, because data on race, language spoken at home and ancestry identification is available down to the census tract level. However, the census only comes out every ten years. We need to look for other sources to keep up with constantly changing figures. We are fortunate to have the New York City Department of City Planning, which collects and analyzes immigration statistics for New York City and publishes the *Newest New Yorkers* report every five years. Data given in the appendix tables is tabulated in a way that can be easily related to our branch service areas. Other city agencies may not have any demographic products released on a regular basis, but have useful data in their databases. In cases like this, we have to be more aggressive in contacting the agencies, finding out what they have and submitting formal requests for customized jobs to be done for us. Although there may be many phone calls, e-mails or faxes back and forth, the moment of receiving the data that we have been looking for is most rewarding.

Since the hiring of our first Information & Data Analysis Librarian, we have published five demographic studies. The first two reports were based on the 1990 Census. *An Ethnic and Language Profile* presents data on the racial/ethnic and language characteristics of Queens residents. The second report, *A Profile of Demographic and Social Characteristics*, includes the number of people who lived outside the fifty states of the U.S. before April 1, 1985. The tables in this report include, for each source country, data on sex, race, Hispanic ethnicity, citizenship status, age, employment, occupation, industry, education, living arrangements and economic situation. These two reports have been very useful reference tools, especially when they were first published in 1995, because they gave the total population for each branch service area for the first time. Although these figures are now ten years old, they are still being widely used, as they are the only official statistics on total population available at the neighborhood level. These statistics can also be found on the library's home page at

RANKING	COUNTRY	NUMBER	PERCENT	RANKING	COUNTRY	NUMBER	PERCENT
1	China, Total	27,579	11.49	21	Iran	1,989	0.83
2	Former Soviet Union	21,540	8.97	22	Former Yugoslavia	1,845	0.77
3	Dominican Republic	20,554	8.56	23	Egypt	1,812	0.75
4	Guyana	17,497	7.29	24	United Kingdom	1,784	0.74
5	India	14,147	5.89	25	Guatemala	1,523	0.63
6	Colombia	11,901	4.96	26	Israel	1,389	0.58
7	Jamaica	10,602	4.42	27	Brazil	1,182	0.49
8	Philippines	9,951	4.15	28	Honduras	1,116	0.46
9	Ecuador	9,230	3.84	29	Vietnam	1,088	0.45
10	Bangladesh	8,905	3.71	30	Nigeria	1,054	0.44
11	Korea	8,478	3.53	31	Mexico	1,034	0.43
12	Poland	6,478	2.70	32	Japan	724	0.30
13	Ireland	5,965	2.48	33	Canada	713	0.30
14	Pakistan	5,542	2.31	34	Italy	679	0.28
15	Trinidad & Tobago	5,478	2.28	35	Barbados	561	0.23
16	Peru	5,330	2.22	36	Yemen	530	0.22
17	Haiti	4,959	2.07	37	Ghana	489	0.20
18	Romania	3,298	1.37	38	Panama	387	0.16
19	El Salvador	2,640	1.10	39	St. Vincent & Grenadines	226	0.09
20	Afghanistan	2,182	0.91	40	Grenada	199	0.08

Table from study entitled, "International Migrants to Queens: Immigrants Admitted from Top 40 Source Countries, 1990–96," published by the New Americans Program, Queens Borough Public Library in 2001.

http://www.queenslibrary.org, under "The Branch Libraries" or "Discover Queens, New York".

To complement the census data, we have used statistics from the New York City Department of City Planning. The demographic study, *Immigrants Admitted From Top 40 Source Countries Citywide, 1990–94*, helps us to locate the newest immigrants, for example, those from the Former Soviet Union, as many of them came to the U.S. as refugees after the fall of the Iron Curtain. Since the Department of City Planning recently released the figures of immigration to NYC for the 1995–96 period, we have recently completed a new study providing an update on immigration to Queens from 1990–96.

Children and teenagers have always been one of the library's major target groups. Children coming from other countries may need more help using libraries. In order to reach out more effectively to them and their families, we obtained data from the New York City Board of Education on Limited English Proficiency (LEP) Students in the public school system in Queens. Based on the school year 1992–93 statistics (the most current data available at that time), we published *A Profile of Limited English Proficiency Students in the Public School System* in 1995. This study proved to be useful as it tells our CLASP (Connecting Libraries and Schools Project) librarians or branch librarians the language background of the young customers in each of our branch service areas. CLASP outreach activities or parenting programs were designed to accommodate their needs as well as the needs of their parents. We hope to work with the New York City Board of Education to obtain more current statistics in order to publish an updated LEP report.

Our latest demographic study, *Births to Foreign-born Mothers, 1997*, is a new attempt. The New York City Department of Health keeps track of the city's birth records, including mother's country of origin and zip code of residence. With the customized work done for us, we were able to compile the data into a study that

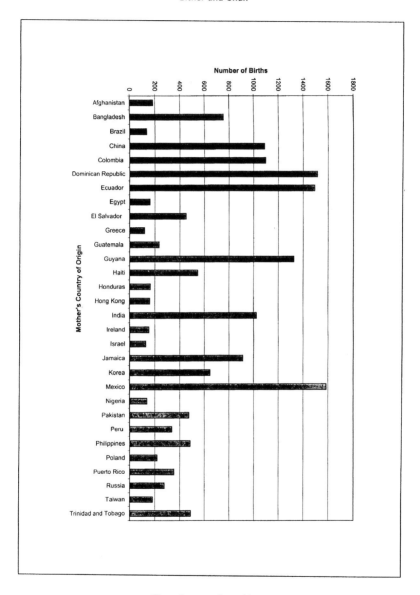

Chart from study entitled,
"Queens Borough Public Library Service Areas: Births to Foreign-born Mothers, 1997,"
published by the New Americans Program, QBPL in 2001.

reveals our potential customers' ethnic background and location of highest concentration for each group. This information is very valuable in assisting the library in designing programs and services for both children and their parents.

In addition to compiling the demographic data into tables, we also use Geographic Information Systems (GIS) software to present data in the form of digitized maps. As all the data that we use has some kind of geographic element, like census tracts or zip codes, thematic maps can be created with the use of GIS software. The advantage of this is, instead of reading through columns and columns of figures, we can now combine the demographic data with our branch locations, branch service area boundaries, highways, transit lines or other public facilities and display them on one single digitized map. At a glance, people can, depending on the data represented, quickly tell the settlement patterns of new immigrants, or which neighborhoods have the most people living below the poverty line. The visual impact is especially good for presentations.

Looking toward the future, we are very excited about the 2000 census. It is the first time in American history that residents have been allowed to check more than one racial category on the census form. If the Census Bureau is going to have all the racial combinations tabulated, this would be the most valuable and accurate data on racial makeup at the local level. Together with information on language, age, income, educational attainment, etc., we expect to complete a number of demographic studies or special projects right after the release of the Census 2000 products. If possible, we would like to use GIS to compare the concentration of immigrants by neighborhood with that of our library cardholders and see to what extent they are using our library. More extensive and aggressive outreach programs could then be designed to reach out to the specific ethnic groups that have lower numbers of library users. While finding the best way to tabulate and make sense of this multi-layered data in relation to our service areas is definitely a big challenge, we are more than happy to embrace it since accurate, specific and up-to-date data is the backbone of quality library service for all.

The Queens Borough Public Library is committed to providing the best customer service to all of Queens' diverse populations. The efforts, both current and future, of the New Americans Program in the area of community analysis will help ensure the success of QBPL's mission. By targeting programs and services using continually updated results of community analysis, we will provide equity of access and help maintain our status as the U.S. library system with the highest annual circulation well into the twenty-first century.

CONEXIONES

SERVING THE INCARCERATED
HISPANIC INMATE

BY STEPHAN LIKOSKY

The New York Public Library has a long history of serving Hispanic and Spanish speaking patrons. Among its current services are Spanish language print and nonprint materials, a wide range of programming both in Spanish or on Hispanic cultural themes, the translation of library brochures into Spanish, English-as-a-Second Language classes, Hispanic book lists, access to the library's Internet home page for Spanish speakers, Internet instruction in Spanish, and the designation of a branch library to house the Hispanic Heritage Collection.

The library's commitment to serving Hispanics extends as well to service to the incarcerated Hispanic population. According to New York State Department of Correctional Services statistics, Hispanics make up close to one third of the approximately 70,000 inmates incarcerated in New York State prisons, and 35 percent of New York City jail inmates. One in ten has Spanish as his/her dominant language. Eighty-four percent of Hispanic inmates in the state's prisons come from New York City. Their ethnic heritage reflects a wide range of origins: Puerto Rican, Nuyorican, Dominican, Cuban, and Colombian, among others. The "typical" Hispanic inmate in the NYS correctional system is male, 34.6 years of age, with a 6th grade reading and math level. Among its services, The New York Public Library's Office of Community Outreach Services, aided by grants from the New York State Education Department, has introduced Spanish language programming into the correctional facilities, and Spanish language materials, which reflect the diversity of Hispanic groups behind bars. More recently, The New York Public Library has translated and distributed its booklet, Conexiones (Connections), which specifically targets the Spanish-speaking ex-inmate or inmate, throughout the correctional system and in the community.

Connections is both a directory of resources in New York City which can be of use to the ex-inmate, and a step-by-step guide to job hunting. It targets those with fewer job-related skills, a criminal record, and if relevant, a history of substance abuse. The first half of Connections is a directory of agencies arranged in fifteen subject categories, such as: ex-offender organizations, education, housing, legal services, addictions, and social and cultural resources. For each agency, there is a current address and phone number, a description of the services offered, eligibility requirements, which languages other than English are spoken by staff, accessibility to people with disabilities, etc. Almost all of the services listed are free. In the second half of Connections, called "The Job Search," there is information and advice on how to prepare for a job. It includes assessing one's skills, writing resumes, and interviewing, as well as advice on how to present one's time incarcerated when applying for jobs, explanations of ex-offenders' rights, and ways to avoid discrimination. The English edition was conceived in 1982, after a survey of correctional facilities regarding the informational needs of the many inmates (upwards of 70 percent) who return to New York City upon release. It was an immediate success, and in 1986, funding was obtained through a private grant to produce the booklet in Spanish. Budget cuts did not allow another edition in Spanish to appear until 1998, and an updated edition is presently under consideration.

The main concerns in producing the Spanish language edition were that it be easily understood by the majority of Hispanic inmates who depended primarily on the Spanish language in their everyday lives, and that it be sensitive to whatever cultural differences might exist between the Spanish and English speaking populations.

Use of appropriate language, needless to say, was critical. The translator we chose for the second edition was a Chilean with proven translation skills and some experience in the field of social services. An editorial committee, composed of a Dominican American, a Puerto Rican, a Cuban American, and myself, was set up to review his work. We decided to use popular vernacular wherever possible, but only when it was correct usage. For example, although it is common to see the sign *librería* referring to "library" in the correctional facilities, *biblioteca* is the correct translation for library, (*librería* means bookstore, in spite of its misleading English cognate.) The translator's choice for "senior citizens," *personas de tercera edad*, was rejected as not commonly understood in New York, and replaced by *personas mayores* (*personas de edad avanzada* and *ancianos* were other options.) In 1983, at the time of the first Spanish language edition, the current word for "drug addiction" was the cumbersome *farmacéutico-dependencia*. In this case, we employed *drogadicción*, which later emerged from unofficial street language to standard usage. Another dilemma: if "inmate" were to replace "convict" in English as a more sensitive, if sugar-coated choice, what would be the best word in Spanish—*recluso*, *presidiario*, *prisionero*, or *convicto*? Popular opinion dictated use of any of the first three, while avoiding *convicto*, which has the harshness of the English "convict." *Ómnibus*, and *autobús*, or simply *bus* were chosen over the word *guagua*, which means public bus to many Hispanics in New York, but sounds like baby-talk, or designates a type of insect to other Spanish speakers.

A more serious challenge regarded the dissemination of HIV/AIDS information. How do we reach Hispanic male inmates, for example, who do not identify themselves as gay or bisexual, yet have sexual relations with other men? In many Latin countries, men define their sexual orientation not so much by whom they sleep with but by what they do in bed. Thus, a male may have sexual relations with another male and still maintain a strong or exclusive heterosexual identity. Persons in this category might never pick up information addressed specifically to gays or bi-

sexuals, yet be every bit as much at risk and in need of information
or services. Some community agencies recognized this cultural
difference early and have started to produce literature addressed
to one or more of the following groups: gays, lesbians, bisexuals,
men who have sex with women and other men, persons of trans-
gender experience, and questioning youth. With the high level of
HIV/AIDS infection in New York State prisons, being aware of
and acting on such a seemingly small cultural nuance could mean
life or death.

For the Spanish language edition of *Connections*, we also included, in the introductory pages, a short tribute to the Hispanics
of New York including their history and contributions. In the directory, we added two Internet sites for resources and information
on Latino cultural and musical events in the city. There were also
additional listings for Spanish language bookstores, and employment, educational, and health programs targeting Hispanic groups
or communities.

To publicize the booklet, we sent copies to all of the ex-
offender and employment-related services listed in the directory.
We also distributed copies to all of the pre-release centers of the
prisons throughout the state, with a flyer, which could be posted
in the general and legal libraries telling of its availability. Each
week the library receives well over one hundred individual requests from inmates, as well as requests for multiple copies from
community organizations, and parole and probation offices, many
of which use the booklet for staff training. There has also been
some publicity in the press.

Fortunately, the task of producing good quality and relevant
services to the Hispanic population in New York is made much
easier by ready access to Hispanic persons themselves. Invaluable
input was obtained in my endeavors from co-workers at The New
York Public Library, representatives of community agencies, and
inmates working at pre-release centers or visiting our correctional
libraries. By mail and in person, many were anxious to share their
suggestions regarding *Connections*. As the Hispanic communities

of New York continue to expand and diversify even further, it will
be a welcome challenge to design and implement library services
to better serve this vital and so often forgotten segment of our
population.

Stephan Likosky, Correctional Services Librarian, Office of Community
Outreach Services, The New York Public Library and assistant Nanabanyin Moses
delivering library services at Riker's Island jail

CONNECTING WITH THE KHMER COMMUNITY

By Brigid A. Cahalan

Thirty-four public libraries dot the Bronx, one of the three boroughs served by The New York Public Library. Good-sized communities of Irish, Italian, Puerto Rican and Jewish descent, formed decades ago, still populate the borough. In addition, a lively mix of immigrants from the Dominican Republic, Bangladesh, the former Soviet Union, and dozens of other countries add to its dynamic flavor and help make it a culturally-rich place to live and work. As Community Outreach Specialist for the libraries in the Bronx, I enjoy working with these groups by coordinating book purchasing in languages other than English, participating in program planning, and reaching out to ethnic community organizations to spread the happy word about the library and its ever-growing repertoire of services.

Our borough can claim the third largest Cambodian community in the U.S., after California and Lowell, Massachusetts. These are the families who fled Pol Pot, Cambodia's murderous leader from 1975–1979. The Federal 1985 Resettlement Act placed refugees from Communist Vietnam and Cambodia in California and Utah and many later migrated to the Northeast seeking industrial work. Several factors precipitated the move to the Bronx—closing of factories in Lowell, Massachusetts; the availability of cheap housing; and efforts of nearby Nyack College and local community-based organizations to resettle the immigrants here.

Almost all the Cambodians are Buddhists. A nearby temple operated by the Khmer Buddhist Society is the spiritual and cultural heart of the community, offering classes in Khmer language for children and adults, music and dance programs, and help and support for their newest families in addition to religious ceremonies. St. Rita's Center for Immigrants and Refugees, opened in 1983, provides English classes and counseling by Cambodian caseworkers, as well as help with finding jobs and housing and securing public assistance, if necessary. Local stores sell Asian food products and one Cambodian store carries Khmer language periodicals, CDs and videos.

About a year ago, after seven years doing outreach work in the Bronx, I found myself pondering the Cambodian population living within two miles of my office in the Fordham section of the Bronx. Although our library offers ESOL classes at many sites, including the Fordham Library Center, few Cambodians had participated. I peered at the small shelf of Khmer language books in the Fordham Library downstairs and resolved to explore possible ways we as a library could develop a closer relationship with and better serve this group.

I began by surfing the Web for some background information on Cambodians and good sources for materials. Towards the end of an unrewarding session, I struck gold with a site produced by the Center for Language Minority Education and Research of the Pacific Southwest Regional Technology in Education Consortium. Besides links leading you to all things having to do with Cambodia, Cambodians in America, and the Khmer language, you find lists of recommended bilingual English/Khmer books (mostly folktales), books in English on Cambodian culture, dictionaries, and some nonprint materials. The distributors listed, with live links, were Pan Asian Publications, Multicultural Distribution Center and Shen's Books and Supplies. Bayon Market Multicultural Center in Long Beach, California, was described as "the best source for pure Khmer literature," so I requested a catalog. When it came, I was delighted to see how extensive and user-friendly it was. Item listings are given in the original Khmer script, with the English transliteration and an English translation for each, making it convenient for both Khmer and English speakers to use. Excited by this discovery, I was keen to find Khmer speakers to help select materials.

A directory of New York City services to immigrants pointed to several organizations serving Cambodians, including CAAAV (formerly called the Committee Against Anti-Asian Violence). Since I had read about CAAAV in the local papers and knew they keep their finger on the pulse of Asian immigrant concerns, I gave a call. Soon the head of their Youth Leadership Project made the trip from Manhattan's East Village with a young Cambodian woman from the Fordham area, and we met in my office. It was fascinating to hear about the work their Project has done teaching teenagers and young adults the skills to successfully mobilize and work toward improvement, issue-by-issue. They passed on the name of Mr. Leang Lang, the president of the Khmer Buddhist Society, which is headquartered a few blocks away from the Fordham Library. Upon speaking to Mr. Lang, I sensed a man of spirit and action who would be a choice ally in this project. We met shortly after; he gave me insight and information, and agreed to study the catalog and select what he felt would be the most useful items for the Fordham Library. The Head Librarian of the Fordham Library, Elga Cace, had expressed enthusiasm for adding to the Khmer collection, so we forged ahead and ordered slightly fewer than 100 items from Bayon Market. The topics he selected included learning Khmer, cookbooks, poetry (including bilingual editions), Khmer literature, Cambodian culture and traditions, sociology, and history. Several of the books selected were in English on Khmer history and tourism. He told me that books on Khmer Buddhism were not necessary, since the community has access to a good selection of books on this topic at the nearby temple.

One of the librarians working at the Fordham Library, Hong Yao, was particularly eager to have Fordham host a program on Cambodian culture. Having come from China as an immigrant herself, Hong knew the importance of celebrating culture. She joined Mr. Lang and me in our next meeting to start planning. He examined the stage in the modest auditorium, and promised to arrange a music and dance presentation for the space. We felt traditional Khmer refreshments would be a nice touch and suggested a local Asian market might provide perhaps tea and small finger treats. Mr. Lang agreed and not much more was said about that aspect. In future meetings, we decided on text and a picture for the flyer and Mr. Lang gave us a beautifully-produced translation in Khmer for the flyer verso. Since the performers were part of the Khmer Buddhist Society, they were most happy to perform for the local community and asked for a very modest honorarium. This would be paid for by the New York State Coordinated Outreach Services Grant. Several hundred copies of the flyer, which was duplicated in a bright orange, were distributed throughout the neighborhood and mailed/faxed to organizations serving immigrants and refugees throughout the Bronx and other parts of New York City.

We arranged an exhibit of books about Cambodia from the children's, young adult, and adult collections of the library in a prominent display case. At the center was a poster of a larger-than-life Cambodian beauty, in the style of a travel agency poster, beckoning patrons into the Cambodian American world. A stuffed rabbit was borrowed for the exhibit and perched above a copy of *Judge Rabbit and the Tree Spirit*, a familiar tale from Cambodian folklore. The background for the exhibit was swathes of blue cloth, as blue is one of the colors of the Cambodian flag.

The day of the program—August 26, 2000—was soon here. Hong and I brought a selection of library-related information to the auditorium and were ready to help out, perhaps serving tea. An hour before the scheduled start, teenage boys and women carrying pots started arriving with Mr. Lang. The boys were mobilized to set up the room—tables and chairs were moved with ease; paintings of traditional Cambodian landscapes were hung on the wall; and valuable pieces of furniture and decoration were placed around the room to provide a total atmosphere. Although I've never been to Cambodia, I felt like Cambodia was coming to me. Then we started becoming aware of the enormity of the feast that had been prepared. Two long tables were filled with steaming pots of rice milk with Khmer noodle soups, crispy spring rolls, fried rice with lots of delicacies, and tasty coconut milk with a special rice dessert. The audience filed in; the room was soon filled and chairs were brought from everywhere. Most were Cambodians, but there were a number of others as well.

Cambodian dancers performing at the Festival of Khmer Culture at Fordham Library Center, The New York Public Library in August 2000
Left to right: Somaly Sophuok, Chhaya Chhoum, and Solida Por. Photo by the author

Ms. Yao began the program by introducing Mr. Lang, who proceeded to welcome the crowd in Khmer and English. Three young women in exquisite traditional dress performed several dances, and impressed all with their meditative movements and graceful and evocative hand motions, so characteristic of Cambodian dance. They left to wild applause. The string musicians we had been expecting were unavoidably detained, so the multi-talented Mr. Lang pulled out the wooden flute which he had played since childhood and treated us to a few tunes, giving cultural details as he performed. Men in Cambodia play the flute to lift their spirits and the spirits of those around them, and the strains were often heard in the refugee camps of Thailand where most Cambodians stayed before resettlement. This was truly a multi-sensory feast—after our eyes and ears were feasted, the eating began!

The teamwork was impressive—after the delicious food was eaten, cleanup was efficient and thorough. The audience was one of the largest and happiest that had ever come to a program in the Fordham Library Center. We heard many requests for similar programs in the future and will be planning such events.

Since the local press hadn't shown up, I took some photographs and brought them over to one of the neighborhood papers, which was happy to print one of them on the front page of the next issue.

Working with the Khmer community on these projects has been a delight. I'm eager to pursue and enhance this relationship, and look forward to the day when we have Cambodian staff working in many units of The New York Public Library. The experience has also strengthened my resolve to work more closely with other groups in the neighborhood—Albanian, Bangladeshi, and Vietnamese, to name a few—and take advantage of their valuable help for collection development and program planning.

HISPANIC HERITAGE MONTH

AT SUNSET PARK BRANCH

BROOKLYN

By Dorothy Buice

Multiculturalism is a way of life at the Sunset Park Branch of the Brooklyn Public Library. We serve a neighborhood whose population is approximately 50 percent Hispanic (Puerto Rican, Dominican, Cuban, Mexican, Ecuadorian, Colombian, etc.) and 25 percent Chinese, with the balance a mixture of Irish, Italian, Scandinavian, African American, Middle Eastern, Indian, and others. We are blessed with an international staff that includes librarians born in Jamaica, China, Ecuador, and Russia, as well as clerks from China and India. The American-born staff includes members of African, French, English, Greek, Irish and Italian descent. All of our programs have multicultural participants, and many have content with a specific ethnic focus. Spanish and Chinese materials account for at least 17 percent of our circulation. All three languages are represented in many formats (books, magazines, audio books, book/cassette kits, and videos).

One of our most successful series of programs was our celebration of Hispanic Heritage Month in October of 1999. We had three bilingual story hours for preschool children, culminating with a party. Children's Librarian Gregoria Flores, a native of Ecuador, conducted the programs. She was assisted by Library Associate Maisha Hoskins and Assistant Branch Librarian Dorothy Buice. Ms. Flores read books in Spanish, such as *Con todo mi corazón*, *La pequeña gallina roja* and *Las lechucitas*. The others read the stories in English. Finger plays and songs such as "La mosca" were also performed. Words to the finger plays and songs were printed and given to the teachers. "La mosca" made such an impact with the children that their teachers reported that they kept singing it at the school. After the stories the children did crafts related to what they had read. For example, after singing a song about colors, "De colores," they made objects using different colors of tissue paper. Attendance at the first session was twenty-five, with eighteen attending the second.

The party on the last day featured face painting and refreshments. Daniel Santos of Community School District 15 also read to the children and donated books to each of the participants. Most of the books were in Spanish, although a few were bilingual or in English. Attendance at the party was 110. Approximately 80 percent of the participants were Hispanic. Several groups from area day care centers and kindergartens attended, as well as preschool children and their parents from the neighborhood. All programs were held in the branch meeting room in the basement.

Daniel Santos of Community School District 15 reading to children
during the Hispanic Heritage Celebration at the Sunset Park Branch of
the Brooklyn Public Library in October 1999

The goals of the program were to attract the Hispanic community to the library and to help Hispanic children aged three to five to appreciate and have pride in their Spanish heritage. Ms. Flores planned the program for about a month, with the support of the Branch Manager, Opal Brown Lindsay. Funding for the supplies and party refreshments came from the regular library budget. Ms. Flores designed flyers in Spanish and in English and sent them to neighborhood schools and day care centers. When some of the area day care centers did not make appointments to bring their children, she personally delivered flyers to the centers. A local Spanish language radio station announced it as a community event. Inside the library a large banner saying "Let's Celebrate Our Hispanic Heritage in October" was displayed. The program was listed in the Calendar of Events for the Brooklyn Public Library system.

Since the program was so successful, similar events were planned for the next year. In 2000 the program was even more successful. There were four sessions, with a total attendance of 253. Several day care centers and kindergarten classes in the neighborhood participated, as well as a number of children who came with their parents. The first three programs were bilingual, but the last was in Spanish only, for groups of children who have recently emigrated from Hispanic countries.

The programs were low in cost, with refreshments for the party being the main expense. Similar programs can be done in any library with a bilingual librarian. It could also work using a member of the support staff or the community as an interpreter if a bilingual librarian is not available.

I LIFT MY LAMP
THE NEW YORK PUBLIC LIBRARY
SERVES IMMIGRANTS

By Harriet Gottfried

In the first half of the 20th century waves of non-English speaking immigrants and migrants came to the U.S. mainland and dramatically altered the population of New York City. From 1910 onward, men, women and children from Eastern and Southern Europe fleeing tyranny and poverty made new homes in this major port of entry. Significant migration by Puerto Ricans, in search of better economic conditions, began at the close of World War I and remained steady. In the 1930s and 1940s horrific conditions in Europe again brought a flood of refugees, many of whom also settled in New York City.

The influence of nineteenth-century moralistic philosophies imbued wealthy New Yorkers with a desire to aid in the self-education of the poor. Since 41 percent of the population of New York City in 1910 was immigrants, there was a strong feeling that this self-education must be extended to them. This mission was accompanied by a belief that immigrants must quickly become assimilated Americans. The administration of The New York Public Library (NYPL) regarded themselves as important agents in this process of self-education. New branches were built in the areas most populated by immigrants and librarians were encouraged to build collections of books in other languages. The circulation department publicized these collections in advertisements and booklists printed in many languages that were distributed to settlement houses, churches and schools. The library also hired "foreign assistants" who were fluent in other languages to work in branch libraries. The outstanding work of these staff members launched a golden age of library service to immigrants in the first fifty years of the twentieth century that remains an inspiration and a model.

Although English and citizenship classes as well as easy reading materials were available in library branches, the work of the library staff with non-English speakers was soon driven by a sensitivity to the language and background of those from other countries. Librarians and foreign assistants became committed to a philosophy of cultural pluralism that was exemplified by an astonishing array of special programs designed to reinforce rather than weaken the immigrant's cultural ties. Speaking to neighborhood people in their own languages, foreign assistants invited newcomers into the library where the joys of music, theatre, lectures, and free access to works of literature awaited them. From the early 1900s to the 1950s, a wide variety of Hebrew, Russian, Polish, Czechoslovakian, Italian, German, French, Hungarian, Swedish, Yiddish, Bohemian, Spanish and Chinese "evenings" were held at many branches in Manhattan and the Bronx. At these evenings, concerts and exhibits featuring international music and art were held. Lectures, theatrical productions, and readings of works by established immigrant writers, poets and novelists were conducted in many languages. A reception followed, featuring food from the culture that was being celebrated.

In addition to programming, staff training in working with non-English speakers was ongoing. In 1907, staff attended a meeting at the Tompkins Square Branch where a lecture entitled "Yiddish Popular Street Literature" was given. That same year, a staff meeting at the Webster Branch had Bohemian literature and music as its topic. Training that concentrated on working effectively with the "foreign-born" continued for decades.

As a result of this impetus, neighborhood branches evolved into vibrant community centers. When immigrants entered the library, they were greeted by a staff member who spoke their language, and were encouraged to attend events highlighting their country of origin. A full description of this rich programming heritage would fill several volumes, but the focus here will be on three of these initiatives.

The Mothers' Club at Seward Park

Mothers' Clubs originated in the settlement houses and spread to library branches. In 1916, a Miss Lifshitz, the foreign assistant at Seward Park, on the Lower East Side, established a Yiddish Mothers' Club. From conversations with children who came into the branch, she was aware that neighborhood women lived in unheated coldwater tenement rooms and were overburdened by housework and the struggle to make ends meet. Miss Lifshitz was eager to keep their culture alive and to make them feel at home. The first NYPL Mothers' Club had its inaugural meeting on a cold Saturday afternoon with seven women in attendance. Sixteen women came to the second meeting and thereafter attendance

Yiddish Mothers' Club performance, ca.1931
Photo courtesy of the Seward Park Local History File, The New York Public Library

grew to a high of eighty members. Meetings, conducted solely in Yiddish, were held on a weekly basis. Activities included discussions of current events and stories that were read aloud. Speakers came from the *Daily Forward* and the Jewish Theological Seminary. Yiddish poets, novelists and playwrights came to read their works. There were Hanukkah and Purim parties. Several husbands objected to the time their wives spent at the library, particularly since club members agreed to leave their children at home. This did not discourage Miss Lipshitz, who began taking the women on field trips to The Metropolitan Museum of Art, the Museum of Natural History and to see Molly Picon perform. After Miss Lipshitz' death, the club still continued to meet and was led by Fanny Wlodawsky, a Yiddish-speaking librarian. She obtained tickets to Yiddish plays at reduced rates and took club members and their families to the theater. In 1941 the club held its 25th anniversary, an event that many of the original members attended. Staff shortages, population shifts and the death of Fanny Wlodawsky finally led to the club's demise in the 1950s. Commenting on Miss Wlodawsky's death in her annual report, the Branch Librarian noted, "With her passing goes most of the old Seward Park Library."[1]

Outreach to Puerto Rican Children at 115th Street

Pura Belpré, who would become a well-known children's author, was the first Puerto Rican librarian to be hired by NYPL. In 1929 she was assigned to the 115th Street Branch in a predominantly Puerto Rican neighborhood in upper Manhattan. Ms. Belpré was immediately concerned with bringing the Spanish-speaking community into the library. "One thought was foremost in my mind. How to reach these people...when to some of them the library was a new factor in their lives."[2]

---

[1] NYPL Archives. RG 8. Seward Park Branch. Annual Report, 1954.

[2] Pura Belpré. "Children: the Link between the Spanish Adult and the Library." Pura Belpré Papers.

She began a series of imaginative programs to attract children. Committed to preserving Puerto Rican folklore, she conducted story hours in Spanish, recounting folktales she had listened to as a child. Energetic and enthusiastic, Ms. Belpré visited community organizations to publicize her programs. She used puppetry in her storytelling and later founded a theatre club of children who performed for library and community audiences. Her outreach efforts inspired other staff to encourage Spanish-speaking adults to come to the library by offering programs that featured Hispanic poets, artists, and musicians. Ms. Belpré began an annual branch celebration of "El día de los reyes" (Feast of the Three Kings). For this event she organized stories, music and dance performances for the community. Largely due to Pura Belpré's leadership, 115th Street became a cultural center for the Spanish-speaking community during the 1930s.

The Metropolitan Opera Concerts at Ottendorfer

Endowed in 1884 by Oswald Ottendorfer, a political refugee from Germany, this branch on Second Avenue and Eighth Street, housed an excellent German language collection. Charlotte Hubach, the Branch Librarian for many years, was a leader in the field of German letters. In 1933 Nazism was sweeping across Europe and throngs of German-speaking refugees were brought to New York by the Hebrew Immigrant Aid Society and the International Rescue and Relief Committee. Large numbers of these new immigrants were writers, musicians and artists who were predominantly Jewish, but also included politically active Catholics and Protestants. Having left their material possessions, including books, behind, they came to Ottendorfer where they could read for free.

One rainy Saturday in 1937 Katherine Meyer, a library staff member, observed a group of refugees huddled outside the door of a nearby music store where the weekly Metropolitan Opera concert was being broadcast. The following week Ms. Meyer brought her own radio and invited the group into the library to listen. When Charlotte Hubach observed how the music transported these refugees, whom she knew were consumed with worry for family members still in Europe, she sprang into action. First she convinced one of her more affluent readers to purchase a radio for the library. Then she contacted the Metropolitan Opera, explained about the program and talked the Met into donating free programs, librettos and posters of the performing artists to the branch. The audience of refugees, seeking comfort in familiar music, continued to build and was a weekly event for years. During the intermission, listeners would exchange anecdotes about the Berlin, Vienna and Prague Opera Houses where they had gone to hear concerts. In 1945 Ms. Hubach commented to a reporter: "They love good music...some of them never miss, rain or shine. It is such a small thing to do for them, but a great pleasure. I never intrude on their privacy. We never press them in any way. They are our guests."[3]

Underpaid and overworked, these pioneering librarians and foreign assistants of the past nonetheless found the energy to reach out with dedication, vision and empathy to strangers in a strange land. To the Yiddish women who met together at Seward Park, the Puerto Rican children who attended story hours at 115th Street, and the refugees who listened to the radio concerts at Ottendorfer, they held out a lifeline that connected newcomers to America with the language and culture they had left behind.

BIBLIOGRAPHY

Books

Brown, Frances Eleanor. *Library Service to the Disadvantaged.* Metuchen, New Jersey: Scarecrow Press, 1971.

[3] NYPL Archives. RG 8. Ottendorfer Branch. Early Branch History.

Dain, Phyllis. *The New York Public Library: A History of Its Founding and Early Years*. New York: The New York Public Library, 1972.

Flexner, Jennie. *Making Books Work: A Guide to the Use of Libraries*. New York: Simon and Schuster, 1942.

Garrison, Dee. *Apostles of Culture: The Public Librarian and American Society, 1876–1920*. New York: Free Press, 1979.

Heim, Kathleen M. and Wallace, Danny P., Eds. *Adult Services: An Enduring Focus for Public Libraries*. Chicago: American Library Association, 1990.

Lyndenberg, Harry Miller. *History of The New York Public Library, Astor, Lenox and Tilden Foundations*. New York: The New York Public Library, 1923.

Monroe, Margaret E. *Library Adult Education: The Biography of an Idea*. New York: Scarecrow Press, 1963.

Journal Articles

Hernandez-Delgado, Julio L. "Pura Teresa Belpré, Storyteller and Pioneer Puerto Rican Librarian." *Library Quarterly* 62 (1992): 425–440.

New York Public Library Archives

RG 8. OBL Branch Annual Reports
    Chatham Square
    Hamilton Fish
RG 8. OBL Promotional Papers 1914–1963
RG 8. Ottendorfer Branch. Box 1 Annual Reports: 1924–54.
    Scrapbooks: 1939–53.
RG 8. Seward Park Branch
    Box 1 Annual Reports: Branch Librarian, 1920–55, Foreign Worker, 1940–55.
RG 8. Tompkins Square Branch
    Box 1 Annual Reports: Branch Librarian, 1924–1958, Foreign Worker, 1934–52.
RG 8. Tremont Branch. Box 2 Foreign Work, 1952.

"Circulation Department Staff News", 1902–1910.
"Staff News", 1911–1939.

MORE THAN A MELTING POT

SELECTING BOOKS THAT REFLECT
THE FULL RANGE OF HUMAN DIVERSITY

By Caren Shilling Koh

On July 8, 2000, Queens Borough Public Library presented its publication, *Open the Books and See All the People* at the Office of Literacy and Outreach Services Diversity Fair at the ALA Annual Conference. This publication was the culmination of more than three years of work done by twenty-six children's librarians. The project began as the creation of replacement lists to use in broadening our collections to be sure that, "Queens Borough Public Library has materials for children that reflect the full range of human diversity." It evolved into the creation of a reference resource that is used at our children's reference desks to meet children's needs for school assignments and readers' advisory.

In 1997, a five-member work team met to define what many call "multiculturalism." The term they decided to use, as set out by one of our strategic directions, quoted above, is "Human Diversity." In the beginning, it was assumed that this term referred to racial and ethnic diversity. However, it soon became clear to the work team that Human Diversity meant more than race and ethnicity. Those who have heard the term, "Deaf culture" and other similar terms can attest to the fact that cultures can be formed on bases other than ethnic or racial background. A working definition was developed (see below) and the five-member team became a sixteen-member team plus a facilitator.

The working definition of Human Diversity was as follows:

Illustration by Sean Murtha for *Open the Books and See All the People*
Used with permission of Queens Borough Public Library

1. Physical Appearance and Traits (height, weight, eyeglasses, hair, clothing, left-handedness, etc.)
2. Gender Roles
3. Sexual Orientation
4. Physical Challenges
5. Mental Challenges
6. Learning Disabilities
7. Family Structure (extended families, birth order, single-parent families, stepfamilies, etc.)
8. Family Problems (alcoholism, parent in jail, abuse, etc.)
9. Chronic Illness and Death
10. Racial, Cultural and Ethnic Diversity
11. Languages
12. Religious Diversity

13. Historical and Geographic Settings
14. City/Country Settings
15. Education (levels of education, various learning environments)
16. Socioeconomic Status

The sixteen members of the Human Diversity work team, all children's librarians, were each assigned a segment of the working definition to research. They refined definitions of their assigned segment, then searched for fiction and non-fiction titles that best fit the definition of their segment.

Titles were evaluated by various criteria. They had to be owned by the Queens Library. They had to be in print. In most cases, they had to be of high literary quality. They had to make the reader feel what it was like to be the main character of the book and better appreciate that character's life situation. For example, if a book was set in Africa but only showed animal life on the savanna, it did not qualify as a recommended title for the Human Diversity replacement lists. Once titles were gathered, the work team met to discuss all titles and then refine and finalize the list. This process took about one year and was repeated two more times for a total of three cycles.

To give you an idea of the content of the lists, we have selected two categories of Human Diversity: Racial, Ethnic and Cultural Diversity; and Languages. The final list for Racial, Ethnic and Cultural Diversity presented over 300 titles. These included African and African American (84), Asian American (79), European (54), Indigenous Peoples – USA (44) and Hispanic American (38). There were also several titles for Caribbean Americans and those from the Middle East. Forty ethnic groups were represented including Gullah, Ashanti, Chinese, Korean, Vietnamese, Indian, Hmong, Palestinian, Polish, Italian, Russian, Jewish, Croatian, Norwegian, Roma, Mexican, Colombian, Guatemalan, Bolivian, Puerto Rican, Cuban, Haitian, West Indian, Hawaiian, Eskimo and American Indian. The Languages category included 89 titles, almost all of which were bilingual. Languages represented included

Bengali, Chinese, Haitian Creole, Spanish, Urdu, Hebrew, Korean, and Punjabi, among others.

Languages

Illustration for the chapter "Languages" in *Open the Books and See All the People*
Used with permission of Queens Borough Public Library

The finalized lists were then statistically analyzed to determine the percentage of our sixty-two branches that owned each title. On average, 30 percent of our branches owned each title on the finalized lists. Based on this statistic, it was determined that money was needed to replace titles and replenish the library's collections.

In the first cycle, Strategic Directions funds were set aside from the general budget to give each children's room money to purchase replacement titles from a specified list. In the second cycle, branches were provided with replacement lists and they were expected to budget from their own funds (which were generous that year) to purchase titles from them. In the third cycle, funding was provided by the Carnegie Corporation for the branches to purchase titles from the final set of replacement lists and also for the library to publish the Human Diversity Lists in their entirety as *Open the Books and See All the People,* including a total of 1,723 books.

Since completing the lists, Queens Borough Public Library has continued to search for titles that fit its working definition of "Human Diversity" to broaden its collections. The library's Children's Book Selection Committee highlights "Diversity Titles" each month, which appear in a special section on monthly juvenile order lists. As a result, the librarians in our library system have developed a heightened awareness of what multiculturalism and diversity mean in terms of their customers, who live in one of the most ethnically and culturally diverse counties in the United States. They are aware of new titles that will more readily meet the needs of all children they come in contact with in the course of their work.

Along with the heightened awareness of customers' needs comes the awareness that there is a lack of titles available from the publishing industry to meet them. While there are many books on various cultures in the context of food, cultural festivals and holidays, there is little that portrays everyday life in various cultures. Moreover, lesser-known ethnic groups (Tibetan, Pakistani, Austrian, Malaysian, etc.) and complex social issues (sexual preference, mental illness, suicide, etc.) are barely touched upon or not mentioned at all. It is possible that publishers will see our lists as a market research tool as we urge them to provide products that would appeal to a broader consumer base than they are presently targeting.

Queens Library's director, Gary Strong, says it best in his preface to *Open the Books and See All the People,* in addressing the publishing industry: "It is also my hope that our colleagues in the publishing industry will see this as a call to arms. We need high quality materials for a variety of age and reading levels that address complex social issues. Go out on a limb—there truly is a market out there." The library has sent copies of the published list to regional sales representatives at the major publishing houses and distributors in hopes that they will agree, and has set up e-mail/phone contacts for those interested in purchasing the list (publications@queenslibrary.org; (718) 990–0705).

Since 1997 the work of twenty-six children's librarians in Queens has evolved through several stages. What began as an internal selection tool took on the role of a reference resource. As time went on, it increased in scope and became a selection and reference tool to share with other library systems. *Open the Books and See All the People* is now being employed as a lobbying tool to demonstrate public libraries' need for more diverse materials from publishers. Queens Borough Public Library, in publishing this work, has moved from fulfilling its own mission statement to taking on a mission to speak up for our customers in the national arena. Perhaps its contents will inspire those responsible for materials selection in libraries to evaluate their own collections in relation to their constituencies and, if necessary, adjust accordingly.

MULTICULTURAL MULTIMEDIA
ETHNIC FILM & VIDEO PROGRAMMING

By David Callahan

Media programming can be one of the most effective forms of ethnic service, and it is certainly one of the most enjoyable. As Senior Film/Video Librarian of The New York Public Library's Donnell Media Center, I am regularly involved in the organization of ethnic-oriented film and video programs.

The Donnell Media Center holds the principal film and video collections of The New York Public Library. The library started a film collection in 1953, and this initial acquisition has grown into one of the largest public library collections of its kind in the country. The collection has been built over the years by librarians who have worked in New York's many neighborhoods, people who have developed a keen understanding of their community's tastes and needs. The collection, then, is a reflection of the rich and diverse population the library serves, and a valuable resource for ethnic programming.

The library began multicultural media programming in 1979, and has presented a healthy selection of such film and video programs ever since. Over the past year alone, Donnell has presented Taiwanese, Slavic, Greek, African, Mainland Chinese and Brazilian series. As enticing as our offerings are, however, we have learned that simply putting together an ethnically-oriented series does not guarantee success. Such programming requires thoughtful curation and appropriate promotion and exhibition.

In choosing works for presentation, the following resources may be consulted: *The New York Times Film Reviews*, issued biennially, is valuable not only as a measure of a film's quality but also its availability for programming. The *Times* reviews only films that receive American distribution, and usually (but not always) lists the distributor. *The Motion Picture Guide* provides a review, distribution information, very detailed production credits, a complete description of a film's plot, and a content advisory. Most important for ethnic programming, its index includes a list of films by country of origin. Originally issued as a set covering the silent era through 1984, it was issued annually from 1985 until 2000, when it ceased publication.

The Internet Movie Database (http://www.imdb.com) has the advantage of currency and is searchable by country of origin. It is a bit tricky to navigate though. One must first select "more searches" from the home page, then select "Country" from the "Word Search" menu. Also, the information included here is not always complete and accurate. *Variety International Film Guide* is an annually issued resource that provides an overview of a nation's year in cinema. Arranged alphabetically by country, it describes each listed country's cinematic highlights and provides detailed contact information for production companies, film libraries, archives, and institutes. It also gives a thorough summary of the leading international film festivals. *Film/Literature Index*, issued quarterly with annual compilations, is an excellent guide to review literature, including non-English language periodicals. A drawback is that it does not index by country; one must know the name of a film or filmmaker to find review citations.

While several Media Center staff members are well versed in ethnic cinemas, we have found it helpful, on occasion, to consult someone for program advice, typically a person whose ethnicity matches the program's and preferably someone who works in media. For our Greek and Chinese series, for example, we were able to hire guest curators. Besides having a superior knowledge of media activity in their own communities, the curators assisted us in securing screening copies of films and videos and finding guest speakers (filmmakers, in several cases). They also recommended related program events and offered worthwhile tips on how to publicize the series.

With or without outside assistance, however, there are certain key things to consider when putting together an ethnic film/video series. When organizing any media program, it is essential to preview a film or tape before selecting it for presentation, to make sure that the content is suitable and that the film or tape itself is of good, presentable quality. Keeping in mind that the program should be accessible to people both within and outside of the program's ethnic focus, one should also check for clear, easily-read subtitles. If presenting on videotape, check to see whether the tape has been recorded in the NTSC, PAL or SECAM mode. Tapes that are not American in origin will likely not have been recorded in the American standard NTSC mode, and it may be necessary to rent a multistandard VCR to play non-NTSC cassettes.

Speakers who introduce, discuss, or simply field questions from an audience always enhance a program, but besides the obvious need for a familiarity with the selected works, the speaker should also be familiar with the community s/he is addressing. Selecting someone from within the community is always a plus, and it is highly advisable—and culturally sensitive—to have a translator on hand, if needed. The translator would ideally be someone connected with the event, but a local community center should be able to recommend a quality translator.

Once a program has been arranged, the next step is publicity. Contact local area organizations that serve the ethnic group(s) you're trying to reach, as well as schools that offer ethnic studies courses. Alert them to your program and send them program announcements—in English and the language of the ethnic group—for posting and distribution. Contact newspapers or newsletters and radio/television stations of the community you're targeting. Ask them to make announcements about the program, but also invite them to cover the program as a news event. Such coverage can make the difference between a program met casually and one received with great interest. In alerting the local Chinese press to our Taiwanese series, for instance, we found several reporters highly receptive to the idea of writing about it. Several pieces appeared about the presentation and the series attracted large numbers of people from the Taiwanese community, many of whom were new to our branch.

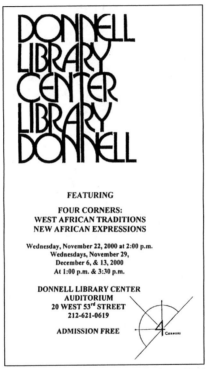

DONNELL LIBRARY CENTER LIBRARY DONNELL

FEATURING

FOUR CORNERS:
WEST AFRICAN TRADITIONS
NEW AFRICAN EXPRESSIONS

Wednesday, November 22, 2000 at 2:00 p.m.
Wednesdays, November 29,
December 6, & 13, 2000
At 1:00 p.m. & 3:30 p.m.

DONNELL LIBRARY CENTER
AUDITORIUM
20 WEST 53rd STREET
212-621-0619

ADMISSION FREE

Front cover of the program for one of the successful multicultural film series presented by Donnell Media Center, The New York Public Library

Other considerations accompany ethnic programming. Over the past year Donnell has presented series of works from both Taiwan and The People's Republic of China. It was important in handling these events to be aware of how the political conflict between Mainland China and Taiwan manifests itself in the local

Chinese communities. In publicizing the Taiwanese series, for example, we were careful to contact newspapers that catered specifically to New York's Taiwanese community, rather than just sending out information generally to the Chinese language press.

Ethnic film and video programming, when presented successfully (invariably a reflection of the effort that went into it), has proven to be mutually beneficial. It offers members of an ethnic community programming it appreciates and recognizes as its own, and it brings potential new users into the library. At Donnell, we have found it to be among the most rewarding types of programming, because it is educational, entertaining, and it further enriches our understanding of the many cultures that make up New York City.

MULTICULTURAL PROGRAMS
IN BEDFORD-STUYVESANT AND BUSHWICK
1999-2000

By Thomas W. Brogan

In 1999-2000, I coordinated three musical-cultural programs at the Bedford Branch of the Brooklyn Public Library and P.S. 333 in the neighboring community of Bushwick. The program at the latter site was part of CLASP (Connecting Libraries and Schools Project), a collaborative project between schools and libraries to encourage reading and use of the public library. The Bedford community is largely African American and Bushwick is predominantly Spanish- speaking. The three programs were related in content, though some songs were specially selected to emphasize the varying ethnic makeup of the neighborhood. Adult literacy students who had expressed an interest in African American spiritual songs received an invitation to the Bedford programs.

Musicians Arthur Kirmss and Richard White presented the programs, which included vocal and instrumental music in traditional styles from African American and Anglo-American to Hawaiian and early American. A show of artifacts such as a set of large fossilized sperm whale teeth shaped into woodworking tools were on display to give a feel for the seafaring songs from early America. A book display was also set up on seafaring life, soldiers and sailors of African American descent who participated in the American Civil War, and Pacific Island culture.

Mr. White and Mr. Kirmss complemented each other in their historical interest and musical talents. Mr. Kirmss is an American history buff with a specialty in the American Civil War who dons a Union soldier's uniform when he plays Civil War songs. Mr.

White's knowledge of Hawaiian music, along with stories of his correspondence and visits with outstanding Hawaiian musicians, gave the programs a far-reaching "overseas" quality. The Hawaiian artifacts and picture books of native musicians helped the audience understand the people and their traditions, and the widespread popularity and influence of Hawaiian music in the entertainment world. Mr. White plays the *dobro* or slide guitar as a specialty, his repertoire ranging from seafaring songs to Hawaiian dance music. While playing the Hawaiian tunes, appropriately dressed in a Hawaiian shirt, he told us of Jerry Byrd, a great steel guitarist he admires. Mr. Kirmss and Mr. White combined their interest in music and history for a multicultural mix.

Great African American spirituals, such as "Swing Low, Sweet Chariot" were included at the Bedford Branch. Mr. Kirmss sang this song while playing the classical guitar and Mr. White played along with the slide guitar. Selections in the Spanish, Irish, and Hawaiian traditions of America followed. Sailor songs were played to evoke the many African men who sailed on the tall ships of early America.

Also at Bedford, African American roles in the Civil War were emphasized. Arthur Kirmss' great-grandfather fought for the Union in the Civil War, and through him were handed down many battle relics, poems, family stories and sheet music, which were used in the program displays. After the war, Mr. Kirmss' soldier ancestor often visited with a fellow Union soldier of African descent who lived in a one-room house in Weeksville, a free community built by its residents in the 1840s in Brooklyn. Weeksville is a noted landmark today and is located near the Bedford Branch.

Fifth-grade classes at the Bushwick School were treated to a similar program to broaden and enhance their knowledge of American history and culture, as well as to focus on some Spanish language songs from their cultures. Mr. White performed the traditional Spanish song "Las golondrinas" as a slide guitar solo. This song brought smiles to the children's faces when they heard the romantic tone of the song.

At the Bushwick performance, the students were especially curious about the Hawaiian slide guitar. They were also surprised at the upbeat tone of the Civil War songs and were interested in hearing how Richard learned to play the slide guitar. They were amazed at the sense of inspiration and celebration in songs written during the Civil War, which to most people is a somber, serious period. One such song of 1863 was the joyous "Girls At Home" by Henry Clay Work.

The three presentations of American folk songs, along with the artifacts, at Bedford and Bushwick, helped bring the history of various time periods alive. The period costumes further authenticated an historical presence. In all, the presentations proved to be both entertaining and educational.

A musical-cultural program can be replicated in any library with musicians interested in American popular and folk music. They might want to dress in ethnic or period costume, for instance in Hawaiian or Early American dress. Knowledge of student audiences in terms of their ethnic history is also important. Some possible sources of musicians are the New York Folklore Society and local historical societies. Arthur Kirmss and Richard White feel that the success of their programs is in large part due to their awareness of local history and a positive recognition of the cultural identity and ethnicity of the audiences.

THE NEW AMERICANS PROGRAM
FORGING PARTNERSHIPS FOR DIVERSITY

By Fred J. Gitner

One in three Queens residents hails from another country and nearly half of the borough's residents speak a language other than English at home. The New Americans Program of Queens Borough Public Library serves residents whose primary language is not English. Since 1977 we have been working closely with ethnic community organizations to assess local needs, link residents with existing neighborhood and system-wide library services, and create new services.

We have chosen to highlight three areas of our services where newly established or strengthened partnerships have been particularly successful.

(See accompanying chart, p. 168)

Collection Development

Collections of popular books in immigrant languages are distributed to branch libraries based on community need. Recently a new collection of over sixty books in Turkish was established in partnership with two Turkish-American organizations to serve this community. Since there is no U.S. source specializing in Turkish books, one of the organizations offered to purchase materials in Turkey based on the library's selection guidelines and donate them to the library. Materials arrived and were cataloged and available in time for a storytelling program in Turkish, where they were extremely well received. A press release alerted the local media.

Coping Skills Programs

These lectures in a variety of languages present practical information designed to help immigrants adjust to life in the United States. For example, working with SHARE (Self-Help for Women with Breast or Ovarian Cancer), and its division serving the Hispanic community, Latina SHARE, a successful workshop in Spanish on Breast Cancer Awareness was offered. They provided a speaker, distributed over 200 copies of publications in Spanish, and provided referrals. The library provided publicity, a book display in Spanish on women's health and a forum for open discussion where all felt welcome.

Cultural Arts Programs

These programs of ethnic music, dance, bilingual poetry, storytelling and crafts celebrate the cultural heritage of the over 100 nationalities in Queens, promote cultural understanding and attract newcomers to the library where they are introduced to the wide range of free services available. We work closely with the Queens Council on the Arts, a publicly-funded arts organization that provides financial support, assistance with publicity and promotion and technical assistance. Through its Folk Arts Program, they assist in locating local performers and artists from many ethnic communities. We have been able to present a number of very successful joint programs including Festival Latino (1000 attendees), a Chinese Theatre Festival (over 400) and Music and Dance from Bangladesh (250), just to name a few. The library provides a bilingual introduction to the programs, a book display pertaining to the culture presented, and information on related library programs and services. This partnership increases attendance and provides a diverse and appreciative audience.

COMMUNITY PARTNERSHIPS BENEFIT QUEENS LIBRARY'S NEW AMERICANS PROGRAM

How do we find Community Partners?	How Can the Library and Community Partners Benefit Each Other?		
	Collection Development	Coping Skills Programs	Cultural Arts Programs
• Personal contacts (networking)	• Once the need is identified, the Library's mission is to provide materials, programs and services to the target population.	• Help immigrants adjust to life in the U.S., and attract new immigrants to the Library.	• Attract new immigrants to the Library.
• Arts groups, ethnic groups, community service agencies, religious groups, business development groups	• Community groups want materials provided, too, and want exposure for their organization and culture.	• Present practical information on topics such as law, parenting, health, employment, etc.	• Encourage new immigrant groups to interact with established community.
• Attendance at community fairs	• Native language collections give new immigrants "equity" in the library.	• Are presented in the immigrant's native language and make them aware of existing community resources.	• LIBRARY provides book display celebrating featured culture.
• Community press announcements of local events, new shops and restaurants, etc.	• PARTNER can help purchase materials in country of origin, according to Library guidelines.	• LIBRARY provides book display on topic, introduces attendees to available library services.	• LIBRARY and PARTNERS make available information on each other's activities.
• Ethnic media	• PARTNER may make donations/encourage funding to accomplish common goals.	• PARTNERS provide speakers (often free), publicity, audio/visual materials and printed hand-outs on topic.	• PARTNERS help Library identify and book ethnic performers.
• Local information section of general press	• PARTNER and LIBRARY both benefit from publicity.	• PARTNERS refer attendees to other support groups and services.	• PARTNERS help publicize programs.
• Yellow Pages			• PARTNERS provide partial funding, in some cases.

Significant Results:
- Increased awareness of library service among ethnic communities.
- Increased library use by new immigrants.
- Library is seen as a community center open to all.
- Facilitates acculturation leading to greater participation in and contribution to the community.
- Creates enthusiastic new groups of library supporters in the community.

All of these activities have been successful thanks to the New Americans Program's constant efforts at outreach to community organizations, maintaining ongoing contact and sharing information. These efforts can be easily replicated by other libraries in their own community settings according to their own analysis of needs, so that the library is seen as serving all of the diverse groups in a community.

NEW YORK ONLINE ACCESS TO HEALTH (NOAH)

NEW YORK LIBRARIES PARTNER TO PROVIDE
QUALITY CONSUMER HEALTH INFORMATION
IN ENGLISH AND SPANISH

BY KRISTINE ALPI, JANE FISHER, AND PATRICIA GALLAGHER

Introduction

In 1994, four New York City library organizations joined forces to establish a single Web site to provide end-users a place on the World Wide Web to reach reliable consumer health information. The organizations: The City University of New York (CUNY) Office of Library Services; the Metropolitan New York Library Council (METRO); The New York Academy of Medicine Library (NYAM); and The New York Public Library (NYPL) — later joined by the Queens Borough Public Library and the Brooklyn Public Library — had as a goal the development of a Web site which would provide health care information easily accessible and understandable to the layperson. The result was New York Online Access to Health (NOAH).

The growth of Spanish-speaking populations increased Internet access through public libraries, and the pressing demand for consumer health information converged early in NOAH's development. NOAH strove to establish itself as a responsible and authoritative bilingual health information site, seeking to reach an underserved population of Spanish-speaking consumers. Several of the NOAH partners serve areas of New York with large Hispanic populations. High usage in states such as Texas, California and New Mexico was also anticipated. While NOAH is certainly used by librarians and consumers in the United States, the pages also reach health providers and Spanish-speaking communities around the world. As of June 2001, the NOAH site was being accessed approximately 610,000 times each month, with about one quarter of the activity linked to the Spanish pages. More than 5000 Web pages currently link to NOAH.

Background

NOAH began in October 1994 as a demonstration project partially funded by the U. S. Department of Commerce, Telecommunications and Information Infrastructure Assistance Program (TIIAP). The original partner library agencies sponsoring the Web site — CUNY, METRO, NYAM, and NYPL — contributed funds and expertise. The united efforts combined the resources of various types of libraries with health agencies in an effort to offer health information at public-access computers in public locations. In the division of responsibilities for NOAH, The City University of New York assumed responsibility for network and database management and housed the original NOAH staff. The TIIAP funds of $275,000 were matched by CUNY to bring the total project cost to $559,150. METRO, a nonprofit membership organization of libraries and library systems in the five boroughs of New York City and Westchester County, participates by including NOAH in its grants, by publicizing NOAH through its publications and Web site, and by providing NOAH committee representation. The New York Academy of Medicine, a not-for-profit medical society founded to promote the health of the public, and the only medical research library in New York City open to the public, provides staff, who edit topic pages and serve on NOAH steering and content committees. The New York Public Library, a large urban public library system, provides staff who participate in NOAH's selection and review process, and contributes members to NOAH standing committees. The division of responsibilities changed in 2000, and now the New York Academy of Medicine handles the overall Web site management.

Initial grant and matching funds for NOAH were used to hire staff, purchase equipment to run the site, and provide access to the server within the partner organizations. The first staff hired included a creative director, a server administrator, HTML coders, a translator and a medical librarian. NOAH's initial grant support allowed the luxury of employing some full-time and part-time employees to develop a limited number of pages for various health topics. However, as the popularity of the site increased and funding decreased, it became necessary to find other methods of contributing to NOAH's growth and development.

NOAH in the New Millennium

NOAH is directed by two groups composed of representatives from the partner organizations: the steering committee and the content committee. The steering committee meets six times a year, and decides on issues such as the budget, new sponsors, and funding sources. The content committee manages the scope of NOAH, suggests topics based on the needs of the patrons who use the partner libraries, and recruits other librarians to participate in NOAH as volunteer page editors. The site is currently managed by one part-time librarian and many volunteer page editors. Page editors are librarians, library science students or master's degree-level health professionals, and the Spanish content editor is a medical librarian with a degree in Spanish.

The original categories (AIDS, Cancer, Heart Disease and Stroke, Pregnancy and others) were selected because of their importance to the health of New York City residents and all documents were made available in English and Spanish. The original model was to host material on NOAH for voluntary health agencies without Web sites. Since most agencies now have Web sites of their own, NOAH links directly to the information on those Web sites. All of the resources selected for NOAH must be freely available. More agencies are making documents available in Spanish, so NOAH does less translating and focuses on linking to Spanish-language information on reliable sites. Link maintenance is always going to be an issue in a volatile Internet environment. It is difficult to keep up with the flow of new information. NOAH now covers health topics ranging from Aging to Tuberculosis, as well as providing resources on hospitals, support groups and statistics. There are a lot of new areas of health information to cover, especially in the area of genetic testing and genetic conditions like cystic fibrosis.

Certain topics—HIV/AIDS, environmental health, pregnancy, nutrition, diabetes and immunizations—have a wealth of information in Spanish. However, there are other areas on the English side of NOAH that are poorly represented in Spanish, such as cancer genetics and childhood cancer, the eye, and foot and ankle conditions. To illustrate this point, the English page on Eye Health has more than 350 links, while the corresponding Spanish page has only thirty. In order to provide even basic information, the selection standards for the Spanish materials must often be slightly relaxed. Many of the translations are not optimal or culturally appropriate and they often contain typos, but they are linked from NOAH because they represent some of the few items available in Spanish on the topic.

Organizations that produce materials in Spanish must be encouraged to add their materials to their Web sites. The Spanish content editor contacts many organizations about making their materials available online, but with little success. The National Library of Medicine has provided some funding for projects that make consumer health materials in English and Spanish available. Two of the most useful for NOAH links are *Access to Electronic Spanish-Language Patient Education Materials: A Utah Community Project (Acceso electrónico de documentos para la educación del paciente en la lengua española: un proyecto comunitario de Utah)* from the University of Utah and the *New Mexico AIDS InfoNet (InfoRed SIDA de Nuevo México)*. Spanish content development is driven by what is available on the Web, by the need to match the English content development and by the desire to respond to people who ask for materials to be made available on topics of concern to them. One example of this response is that a number of people, who do not read Spanish but need to provide information in Spanish, have asked that more bilingual materials be identified on NOAH. NOAH has responded by including both the English and Spanish title with the link and adding a bilingual graphic to assist users.

Challenges

Though the disclaimer on each NOAH page clearly states that NOAH personnel cannot answer personal health-related or research questions, the Web site mailbox receives hundreds of questions each month. Many people find it easier and perhaps more reassuring to ask questions of a person rather than passively read that information on a screen. Due to the nature of the Internet and the Spanish content, much of the access and many of the questions sent to our Web site are from outside the United States. It is surprising how many questions come from health care students and professionals looking for clinical information and statistics. Most questions receive a stock response with a list of additional online resources to consult.

Ongoing publicity for NOAH includes regular discussion list announcements about new topic pages, and brochures distributed at library meetings and health fairs. When NOAH had a staff person responsible for public relations, press releases were issued. NOAH hopes to start doing that again with volunteer efforts. In a September 1998 radio interview, the host of the Spanish program "Good Morning Long Island" shared that many of the station's listeners did not have computers and that the availability of NOAH in the public library would be an important point to stress. When there was a full-time creative director, NOAH was well represented by displays at conferences and health fairs. Now, it is up to the publication and promotion efforts of the various partners and individual editors to keep the word out about NOAH. NOAH is almost always mentioned in library articles and discussion list

postings about quality online health information in Spanish or
English. It gets less mention from the mainstream press, which
tends to focus on U.S. government and commercial sites. The
NYPL uses NOAH as a teaching tool in its "Health Information on
the Internet" workshops.

Conclusion

NOAH is an example of a successful collaboration between different types of libraries and voluntary health agencies to use technology to reach a very broad public. Librarians, healthcare workers
and those using NOAH to provide consumer health information
frequently ask about easy-to-read documents and the availability
of materials in other languages, such as Russian, Chinese, and
Arabic. NOAH needs additional editors for both English and
Spanish language pages before branching out to new languages.
As NOAH has moved to a new URL (http://www.noah-
health.org), publicity becomes even more important. NOAH will
focus on its core goals and will continue to promote itself better to
remain well used among the hundreds of online health resources
available today.

RECENT DEVELOPMENTS IN QUEENS
THE GLOBAL VILLAGE
FORECASTING THE FUTURE

By David Cohen

The borough of Queens is home to the most intensive ethnic mix of the whole country. In a population of just over two million, there are significant numbers of immigrants who are somewhat better off than most due to the extensive array of English classes and other programs and services offered by the Queens Borough Public Library. As far as we can see, the New Americans Program (NAP), now more than twenty years old, is working overtime to assist these immigrants, not only in learning English, but also in providing international language collections where appropriate, and offering their excellent Coping Skills workshops.

Looking at the job responsibilities of the Coping Skills Librarian of NAP gives us insight into the successful strategies developed to address the needs of new immigrants in Queens. Coping Skills programs are offered in languages other than English and are designed to help immigrants adjust to American life and culture. Working closely with the various communities, programs and workshops are carefully designed and executed. Further, there is attention given to the need to purchase and maintain collections in various languages, supported by special bibliographies. Literary programs are also prepared in various languages in order to reach broad sections of the community. The concept of the Coping Skills program has proven to be successful in making the library an essential agency in the pursuit of a multicultural agenda.

Outside of the library field, we are indebted to Professor Roger Sanjek, a colleague in the Anthropology Department at Queens College. He has done intensive neighborhood research in the areas of Elmhurst and Corona, two thoroughly mixed ethnic and racial communities. His findings are presented in a recent volume entitled, *The Future of Us All: Race and Neighborhood Politics in New York City* (Cornell University Press, 1998). The essence of the story has to do with bringing people together through various community activities. In the 1960s and '70s, numerous white families left the area, but in the long run enough white families remained, along with the newcomers, to make it a viable multiethnic community, based on coalition-building and goodwill gestures. As a fascinating saga about bringing people together, it's worth our close attention. Lessons to be drawn from this experience will no doubt be useful all across America.

The book includes several mentions of the Elmhurst Branch Library in relation to programming for the Korean community, and demands by local activists for expanded library hours. As Professor Sanjek says: "The most universally supported quality of life concerns in C.D. (Community District) 4 focus on children: the two-decade-long struggle, still not over, against school overcrowding and for more youth programs; white wardens (civic activists) fought for expanded hours of the Elmhurst Branch Library and organized afterschool and summer programs, and the Teen Center. Black wardens ran summer cleanup and sports programs and tutored at the Lefrak City Branch Library. Latin Americans organized afterschool and summer programs; Latin American, Asian and African American candidates ran for seats on the school board and a Chinese woman from Elmhurst was its first member of color." (page 370)

In conclusion, Elmhurst–Corona was transformed from a solidly white neighborhood in 1960 to probably the most ethnically mixed community in the world by the 1990s. The impact on local libraries was epoch-making. In the coming years we look for more extensive developments in multicultural librarianship, based on this model.

SERVING THE RUSSIAN READERSHIP GOING BEYOND THE BASICS

By Irina A. Kuharets

With a little imagination and attention to patrons, librarians can effectively serve their Russian readership. The people Americans generally think of as "Russians" do not form a homogeneous community. They come from different ethnic, religious, social and cultural backgrounds. Immigrants from the former Soviet Union come from fifteen different republics (which today are sovereign countries), speak one or more different languages, and may be affiliated with any of the major world religions, including various denominations of Christianity, Islam and Judaism. The people librarians think of as "Russians" are readers who prefer reading in the Russian language. The majority, but not all, of these readers are immigrants. The public library serves immigrant Russian readers in the difficult period of adjustment to American culture by providing a collection of books in their mother tongue—the language they grew up with and to which they are most accustomed. For first- and second-generation Russian Americans, the public library serves different purposes: teaching such readers about their heritage and bridging the experiences of their own and their parents' or grandparents' worlds.

Since 1990, I have been the Slavic Specialist at the World Languages Collection of the Donnell Library, a central library of the Branch Libraries of The New York Public Library. In that capacity, I have worked with Russian readers to develop the sort of book collection and activities that meet the ever-evolving needs of Donnell's Russian library patrons. Donnell is conveniently located in midtown Manhattan and from that site serves Russians throughout the entire New York metropolitan area. In this article I will share with you some of the programs Donnell offers its Russian-language patrons, as well as the impetus behind these programs. In describing such programs, my aim is to provide librarians with examples upon which they can expand, or from which they can deviate with the ultimate goal of providing their Russian library patrons with the materials and programs that are most useful to them today.

I. The Basics

There are two fundamentals in effectively serving Russian readers. One, offer many titles in all subjects and all forms of literature. At Donnell, we follow the rule that Russians love to read. So we give them books, lots of books, and we keep up with demand. Two, make the library accessible. For example, post library rules and regulations in Russian, create bibliographies and special displays for new Russian titles, best-sellers, and the like, and offer demonstrations of the use of the library's online catalogue.

The extent and variety of a library's collection and the basic services it provides are beyond the scope of this article, but I will devote a few lines to the topic because it is of paramount importance in effectively serving Russian readers today. Russians are an educated readership. Among them are musicians, actors, doctors, engineers, programmers, lawyers, and businesspersons. Many have varied and sophisticated reading interests, but they also have a need for basic information. Immigrants, for example, will want books and videos on learning English and how to become a U.S. citizen. Although Russians are often thought of as highbrow readers of classic literature, today there is a great demand for genre fiction. The demand is largely fueled by the new wave of Russian immigrants, who bring with them an interest in popular books being published in Russia today. After the fall of the Soviet Union in 1991, private enterprise in the publishing industry forged new directions and began offering an unprecedented number of new titles, particularly genre fiction. Romance and detective stories, both written in Russian and translations, are much in vogue in Russia today. Best-selling American authors such as Danielle Steel and Tom Clancy are very popular, as are Russian fiction writers Viktor Dotsenko, Daria Dontsova, Iuliia Latynina and, particularly, Aleksandra Marinina and Boris Akunin.

Several years ago, Donnell interviewed some of its Russian patrons about what they like to read. The responses of four such patrons are representative of the wide variety of reading interests among Russians. A woman in her mid-fifties who visits Donnell World Languages Collection on her lunch hour enjoys contemporary Russian novelists such as Vasilii Pavlovich Aksenov and Iurii Markovich Nagibin, as well as translations of Agatha Christie, Georges Simenon, and Sidney Sheldon. She also borrows books for an older, homebound relative who likes to read classic adventure novels, such as those by James Fenimore Cooper and Alexandre Dumas. A gentleman in his sixties prefers memoirs, especially by performing artists, and books on Russian history. For another patron, a teenage boy who had immigrated a year earlier and is now studying English in high school, history books and historical novels are important. This reader also enjoys Russian art books. A fourth reader, a gentleman in his late fifties, is interested in how Americans think. He reads books on American history, culture and politics. For his wife, this reader selects romance novels by contemporary writers such as Barbara Taylor Bradford.

At Donnell World Languages Collection, we listen to what our patrons tell us about their reading interests and grow our book collection accordingly. Donnell has a little bit of everything, and a *lot* of genre fiction. We are always looking to enhance our book collection and have been fortunate in this regard to benefit from helpful and efficient book dealers and a budget that allows us to add new titles and replacements. As a result, the Donnell Russian collection has grown to approximately 20,000 volumes that reflect a wide variety of readers' tastes and interests. Much more can be said about library book collections and keeping up with readership interest, but I turn now to the Donnell programs that are the focus of this article.

II. Beyond the Basics

The efforts of Donnell World Languages Collection in going beyond the basics in serving our Russian readership are centered around Donnell's "literary evening" programs and, to a lesser extent, the art exhibitions and film viewings associated with these programs. The literary evenings began in May 1997. At that time, Donnell broke new ground in serving its Russian patrons with two presentations, one featuring renowned stage and screen actress Elena Solovei and, a second, featuring three émigré poets, Inna Bogachinskaia, Leonid Bulanov, and Sergei Shabalin. The literary evenings have continued since with great success.

Dramatic Readings

One type of literary program is the dramatic recital — a one-person show in which an actor (often with the aid of a writer and/or producer) gives a dramatic reading of a featured poet's most popular poems, interspersed with details of the poet's life. Such readings are immensely popular in Russia and in Russian émigré communities. During 1998–99, Donnell had the pleasure and good fortune of working with two well-known, award-winning dramatic performers now living in New York City, Elena Stroganova and Ilya Grakovsky. The actors' unique repertoire included Mr. Grakovsky's 1998 reading of poems by Aleksandr Aleksandrovich Blok, commemorating the 118th anniversary of Blok's birth; Ms. Stroganova's performances included dramatic readings from works by Vladimir Mayakovsky, and a literary composition based on Mikhail Afanasevich Bulgakov's famous novel *The Master and Margarita* and his correspondence.

Patron-Assisted Programs

Several of our Russian readers offer to help with library activities. A number of Donnell's programs were undertaken at the suggestion of such volunteers. For example, shortly after famed Japanese film director Akira Kurosawa died, one of our long-time patrons, Fedor Dobronravov, showed us a portfolio of Kurosawa's drawings. Mr. Dobronravov was a cameraman on Kurosawa's Academy Award-winning feature film "Dersu Uzala" (1974), which was filmed in the Soviet Union. At Mr. Dobronravov's suggestion, the Donnell Media Center showed the film with English subtitles and exhibited drawings and several photographs of the making of the film. At the showing, Mr. Dobronravov made introductory remarks that were translated for the English-speaking audience. Another library patron, prose writer Pavel Lemberskii, helped organize a reading that featured winners of the "Setevoi Broadway – 2000" contest for the best works in Russian about New York. The readers, Irina Mashinskaia (poet), Vadim Iarmolinets (journalist), Vladimir Solovev (prose writer), and Mr. Lemberskii himself, read from their works and answered questions from the audience. Mr. Lemberskii was familiar with Donnell's literary evenings because he had previously received a warm reception from a Donnell audience when he read them excerpts from his new book, *Reka-7.*

"Pushkin is Our All"

One of the most successful literary programs at Donnell's World Languages Collection was its June 8, 1999 gala celebration of Aleksandr Sergeevich Pushkin's 200th anniversary held at the Donnell Bankers Trust Auditorium. Pushkin is Russia's greatest cultural treasure. There is a famous saying of unknown authorship that

"Pushkin is our all." This became the mantra for the Pushkin celebration, which opened with introductory remarks by translator and Slavist Barry J. Rubin, and a talk by literary critic and well-known Pushkin scholar Nadeshda Semenovna Braginskaia. The celebration continued with dramatic readings by Ms. Stroganova and Mr. Grakovsky and an operatic performance by soprano Irina Mozyleva, who sang Russian romances set to Pushkin's poems. *My Pushkin*, a collection of engravings by renowned Russian artist Ilya Shenker, who now resides in New York City, was exhibited at the Donnell Library Center in connection with the celebration. The artist's subtle feeling for Pushkin's poems is reflected in his illustrations and enhanced the atmosphere of joy for our library patrons.

"There was a genuine love for Pushkin that was felt by everyone," said Ms. Stroganova afterwards. After exciting the audience with her passionate speech entitled *On Pushkin*, Mrs. Braginskaia said: "All I can do is to thank the organizers. For two hours, in the center of New York, I could be with Pushkin. There is no more joy than this for me — to be with Pushkin."

1799-1999

Logo used on cover of Russian/English program flyer
for the celebration of the 200th anniversary of the birth of A. S. Pushkin
held at the Donnell Library Center in 1999

The Pushkin celebration was the first in a series entitled "Summer Celebration of Russian Literature," supported by the New York Council for the Humanities and the National Endowment for the Humanities. Two programs that followed celebrated the writings of Ivan Sergeevich Turgenev (1818–1883), Isaak Babel (1894–1940), and Vera Mikhailovna Inber (1890–1972). Each of these programs began with presentations in English on these authors' legacies. In addition to an introduction by Mr. Rubin, the programs consisted of theatrical performances by Ms. Stroganova of the New York Russian Drawing Room Theater. Accompanied by a pianist and violinist, Ms. Stroganova presented two memorable compositions, "Selections from Turgenev" and "Odessa Stories," which featured music by classic Russian composers and instrumental arrangements of the Russian folk song "Oh, Nastasia," Jewish folk songs, and dance music. In a subsequent comment on these programs, Mr. Rubin remarked:

> "It was an honor for me to participate, and I must also say that   I personally derived great esthetic pleasure from all three events. Dramatic performances with their musical support represented Russian culture at its very best. They fully met the highest standards of art that one expects in New York City. From my own observations and from the feedback I received, it is clear to me that the programs were deeply appreciated not only by the Russian-speaking audiences but also by the considerable number of those without Russian, because the artistry of the performers was universally understandable."

Get the Word Out

In the past three years, the Donnell World Languages Collection has hosted nineteen programs focused on Russian literature and culture. Dramatic recitations and programs featuring music had

the largest attendance. Russians yearn to hear classic literary
works read by renowned performers, and musical programs appeal to an even wider audience by reaching out to non-Russian
speakers. Advertising plays an important role in bringing readers
to the library and to our programs. Besides being printed in The
New York Public Library's monthly publication, *Events*, information about our programs is advertised in the Russian daily *Novoye
Russkoye Slovo*, and on a local Russian radio program. Some of the
New York-based Russian periodicals, on their own initiative, publish advertisements taken from our flyers. The flyers are produced
in-house in Russian and English and are sent to all New York
Public Library branches serving Russian communities.

Conclusion

If your library serves a Russian community, I urge you to pay attention to the interests of your library patrons and consider responding with imaginative programs that go beyond basic library
services. I hope the Donnell World Languages Collection programs described in this article serve as a model for the sorts of literary programs your library might consider. Keep in mind that
while our programs have focused on Russian culture and literature, a broad range of topics would be well-received. Some topics
to consider are Russian culture, immigration, citizenship, finding a
job, United States history, and U.S. government.

I leave you with one last idea. The time is ripe for planning a
program around the upcoming tercentenary of St. Petersburg in
2003. Many of Russia's great cultural icons were nurtured by and
are associated with St. Petersburg, including Pushkin, Dostoevsky,
Mussorgsky, Tchaikovsky, Malevich, Chagall, Balanchine,
Nabokov, Shostakovich, and Brodsky. At Donnell World Languages Collection, we have started to gather ideas and plan lectures, book discussions, and theatrical presentations for another
successful celebration of Russian literature and culture in 2003.
The possibilities seem endless.

Serving a Russian readership in a library setting has greatly
enriched my life. I hope your experiences are as wonderful as
mine are. Go ahead. Say *"dobro pozhalovat'!"* (welcome) to the Russians in your community and celebrate their thirst for knowledge
and their vast love of Russian culture!

Participants at the literary evening "Odessa Stories" held on July 17th, 1999 at the
Donnell Library Center. *Left to right*: Viktoriya Spivak, pianist; Felix Yablonovsky,
stage producer; Bella Liberman, violinist; Barry Rubin, translator-Slavist, formerly on
the faculty of Queens College of the City University of New York;
and Elena Stroganova, actress. Photo by the author

STORYTELLING WITH ZENA CHEZA ORIOLLA

By Thomas W. Brogan

Storyteller Zena Cheza Oriolla has a clear, melodic voice. She usually wears a colorful, flowing traditional African-American dress and carries a woven handbag filled with her storytelling props. She believes she can reach all people with multicultural stories because the essence of our common humanity is revealed in folktales that strike a chord with our common spirit.

For Women's History Month in March of 2000, Ms. Oriolla presented a successful multicultural afterschool program entitled "Herstory" at the Bushwick Branch of the Brooklyn Public Library. She spoke about the significance of Women's History Month and delighted the audience of parents and children by telling stories in which women were the protagonists. Then Ms. Oriolla asked for four girl volunteers, whom she dressed in colorful material and headdresses. Each child played a famous woman in history: Queen Mary Thomas of St. Croix, Hatshepsut of Khemet (Ancient Egypt), Queen Nzinga of Angola, and Yemaya (Yoruba goddess of the seas.) As they stepped forward to the audience, Ms. Oriolla narrated a short biography for each woman.

A few months later, in June 2000, Ms. Oriolla enchanted an audience of third graders at P.S. 333, a school neighboring the Bushwick Library, with folktales from around the world. The school librarian, Carrie Schadle, and I arranged this program as part of the Bushwick Branch's Connecting Libraries and Schools Project. Ms. Schadle provided the school's all-purpose room and a third grade audience. Folktales were picked to encourage reading and to help the children learn about stories of other cultures.

For each tale, she invited the children to act out a character or play an instrument. In a Puerto Rican folktale entitled "The Squeaky Bed," the children volunteered to be members of an extended family who shared a large bed. Ms. Oriolla narrated while the children held masks to represent the different characters, e.g., *abuela* (grandmother), *abuelo* (grandfather). Ms. Oriolla gave a mini-lesson in Spanish vocabulary, which was used throughout the story. The rest of the audience vocally imitated a Puerto Rican drumbeat rhythm that reflected the motion of the bed and other instruments. In a West Indian tale with a southern African American twist called "The Dancing Granny," a wise and agile grandmother successfully foils the attempts of Brer Rabbit to steal her crops. The children played the banjo chorus. Ms. Oriolla, in her introduction to "The Dancing Granny" made a connection between Anansi from West African folktales and Bugs Bunny.

A third tale, entitled "Lee Lee Goro," an African story from the Teme people, can be found in the book *Misoso: Once Upon a Time Tales from Africa*. Various animals go on a quest for fire and have to battle a little girl who is under the spell of the Magical Keeper of Fire, Mammy. The children used animal puppets to act out the story, which demonstrated cooperation among the species of the earth. In an African tale entitled "How the World Got Wisdom," Anansi the Spider tries to steal wisdom from the god Nyame. After seeming to successfully do so, the trickster discovers that a small child is far wiser than he. The moral of this tale is that everyone has a share of wisdom.

The mostly Spanish-speaking audience of children seemed to identify most with "The Squeaky Bed," but they also appreciated the tales from other nations. The Puerto Rican students showed pride and excitement in having their country represented. A touching moment was when classmates encouraged one boy who was new to the U.S. and barely spoke English to participate as a character.

Teachers and children complimented the storyteller on her performance. The teachers asked for similar programs in the future since Ms. Oriolla adds a fresh perspective to multicultural storytelling for children. She brings the children into the story by asking them to play a character, play "the banjo chorus," dress a part, or play an individual instrument. In addition, she sometimes teaches the children a few phrases in another language to enhance the story. She also shows through stories how we are all related, whatever our culture, by our universal humanity. By making the stories interactive they become more memorable for the children. Acting out folktales is an excellent way to learn respect and appreciation for other cultures and can be the beginning of a class discussion on other cultures. The children loved Ms. Oriolla's colorful storytelling outfits and responded well to her friendly and gentle style.

If you are interested in dramatizing folktales in your library, first you need to find a storyteller, either a professional or a talented staff member or volunteer. This person should have studied, or should be willing to study, the folklore of many cultures. Familiarity with many of the familiar songs of the target culture(s) is important. They need to think of props to aid in dramatizing the tale. Facemasks can be obtained for children to hold while reciting dialogue and simple costumes can help create a character. Instruments for the children to play can get them involved in the action of the tales. Getting to know the language of a culture is like sharing magic. And don't forget that active participation is the key to making the tales memorable for the children.

To find a storyteller in your area, you may want to contact one of the following:

- African Folk Heritage Circle, (212) 568-1645; afhc96@hotmail.com
- Storytelling Center, (212) 613-3117
- Phyllis Stephens of Peekskill (a good source for upstate storytellers) (914) 788-4642 or (212) 662-7500 x27.

NEWBURGH

NEWBURGH FREE LIBRARY'S BUSINESS RESOURCE & INFORMATION EXCHANGE (BRIX) PROGRAM

By Anne McCarthy Kennedy

Like many public libraries, Newburgh is located just a few blocks from the downtown business "core" of a riverfront city of 27,000. And as in many cities, major employers have closed or moved leaving empty buildings, vacant lots and economic disrepair. Committed to our site in the heart of New York State's largest historic district, surrounded by wonderful architecture and encroaching poverty, we sought ways to integrate the library more intrinsically with the community and to support our neighbors in their enterprises as well as in their ability and desire to support our services. Recognizing that the library had business resources to provide, and knowing that there were business people nearby who rarely entered our doors, we determined to focus on the economic sector of our community to create a new area of service.

In October 1998 we received a Library Services and Technology Act (LSTA) grant through the New York State Library Division of Library Development to fund outreach and programming for small businesses, particularly immigrant and minority entrepreneurs, including women. We intended to partner with businesses, business organizations and resource agencies to assure comprehensive service without duplication, and with local educational institutions to provide experiential learning opportunities to students. And as the Central Reference Library for Ramapo–Catskill Library System, we hoped to develop a model that could be replicated to provide focused business services at other member libraries operating in similar environments.

Simple demographics and developing trends dictated much of
the original planning and decision-making for the program. Small
businesses, defined as those with fewer than 500 employees, comprised over 99.7 percent of employer firms in 1996 (U.S. Small
Business Administration iii). In 1997, 400 new firms started up in
Newburgh, an increase of 0.4 percent ("Newburgh"). Sixty-five to
70 percent of small businesses close within five to eight years
(Nerone). Small businesses comprise the sole economic sector
along Broadway. Most of these are immigrant- or minority-owned,
driven by the large and growing immigrant and minority populations in the city. Women and blacks each own more than 100 businesses in Newburgh; Hispanics more than 100 in Orange County
(U.S. Census Bureau). More precise figures about business owner-
ship demographics would be valuable: we hoped to develop this
information. A study in Great Britain showed that customers tend
to come to the library, and then continue to shop in the neighborhood, rather than the reverse (Linley). So we believed we had a
role to play in stimulating commercial activity. With Orange
County Community College's extension campus and Mt. St. Mary
College located close by, and other educational institutions within
an easy commute, it seemed there would be ample opportunity for
student involvement.

Public libraries across the country have begun to emphasize
business services: Arizona supports a state-wide initiative to provide small business centers in libraries; Danbury (CT) Public Library's Technology Center makes business software and information technology available to customers; Fairfax County (VA) Public Library's Web site offers in-depth research material; Mohawk
Valley (NY) Library Association has set up small business information centers. A study by the Public Library Association revealed
that the majority of larger libraries are active participants in the
Chamber of Commerce (Lynch). Our plans evolved as we met
with representatives from the local Chamber, Kingston–Newburgh
Enterprise Corp., the Small Business Development Center and

others. Focus groups enabled us to learn exactly what the business owners themselves wanted.

At the beginning, BRIX activities were carried out almost entirely by the author, in the position of Business Resource Coordinator, with a small amount of clerical support. Outreach—personal visits to business owners to explain the program, offer services and seek input—involved the additional support of the library's grant writer who was particularly interested in the progress of this initiative.

Many program activities were carried out almost simultaneously. During the outreach phase, the coordinator also met with key individuals in resource agencies, ranging from the Department of Labor through Orange County Community College's Institute for Business, Industry and Government (IBIG) and Orange–Ulster BOCES Entrepreneurial Assistance Program to the Hudson Valley Technology Development Center. A program brochure and bibliography were developed. At the same time, we began individual counseling and referrals as customers inquired about our services.

In April 1999, BRIX sponsored a day of workshops. With support from Key Bank, we partnered with the Rockland Economic Development Center to offer sessions on government procurement and University of Scranton's Electronic Commerce Resource Center Y2K Support Initiative. SCORE (Service Corps of Retired Executives) volunteers and a business consultant conducted sessions on planning for entrepreneurs and home-based businesses. These programs took place in the library's handicapped-accessible auditorium and were free of charge. We used press releases, a mailing to our growing database, flyers distributed through member libraries and word of mouth to publicize the workshops. About fifty individuals attended from all sectors of our target populations: African Americans, Hispanics, Asians and women, with other business owners and professionals participating as well. Our downtown location with its public transportation made these programs widely accessible.

Article highlighting the services of Newburgh Free Library's Business Resource & Information Exchange (BRIX) that appeared in "The Times Herald-Record," Middletown, N. Y., August 4, 1999. Used with permission of "The Times Herald-Record"

It became clear early on that those most interested in accessing our services were Hispanic entrepreneurs, representing many different nationalities. Spanish-language materials were always a focus of collection development along with audio and video business materials and those targeted to African Americans, women, youth, older entrepreneurs and persons with disabilities. In January 2000 we hired a Business Networking Consultant and a Community Liaison to support bilingual outreach and services. From the outset we were assisted and encouraged by the publisher of "El Águila," a bilingual newspaper covering the Hudson Valley. All program materials are now prepared in both English and Spanish; the consultant and/or the liaison provide translation whenever needed in counseling sessions or meetings. As a result, we have been able to facilitate monthly merchants' meetings, largely attended by Hispanic business people, but also including other participants. Each meeting includes a presentation about topics such as business improvement districts, Small Business Administration loans, or taxpayer concerns, as well as time for discussion of local problems and solutions. Hispanic merchants have tried unsuccessfully to establish an association in the past. We hope that the consistency provided by BRIX sponsorship will lead to a realization of this avenue for effective and cooperative business development.

Other program activities cover a wide range. With the pro bono services of an attorney we assisted a Mexican restaurant owner in obtaining a zoning variance. The coordinator, as a member of the Chamber of Commerce Minority and Woman Business Committee, helps would-be entrepreneurs prepare applications for the committee's Microloan and Mentoring Program. We participate in a Business Expo and a Small Business Tabletop Show. Customers have been assisted in finding suppliers of Hudson Valley products, a list of regional labor union chapters, and athletic shoe wholesalers/distributors. The *Buslib-L* discussion list at http://tile.net/lists/buslibl.html, is an invaluable research tool for queries outside the scope of our collection. That list and the *Scout Report* at http://scout.cs.wisc.edu/index.html, are the primary sources for sites added to the *BRIX Web guide*, http://www.newburghlibrary.org/brix.htm, which is continually updated, with annotated links selected and categorized for their applicability to local business interests. The SBANC (Small Business Association Advancement National Center) Newsletter is especially useful in collection development and offers a "Tip of the Week" on a wide range of timely issues. Reference transactions are handled in person, on the telephone, and through fax and e-mail contact. We offer classes in Internet searching and business software applications in the library's E-Learning Center, opened in May 2000 with support from Fleet Bank and member item funds from State Senator William Larkin. And we publish *BRIX BLOCKS*, a current awareness newsletter.

In July 2000, BRIX received the first annual Dun & Bradstreet/BRASS Award for Outstanding Service to Minority Business at the American Library Association Conference. The Newburgh Developers' Association recognized BRIX for its support to the business community in January 2001. What is most exciting is that the program continues to develop services that are both more sharply focused and more extensively accessed by customers from all parts of the library system. Student involvement remains a peripheral concern. One possibility to be explored in the future is mentoring partnerships in which business owners and students can exchange practical experience and textbook knowledge. Our information dissemination role as the Central Library supports member library business services at whatever level seems locally appropriate: distributing materials and notices, counseling and referring clients, researching business queries, etc. We enjoy both the challenge of expanding our own knowledge base to meet their needs, and the success that new and repeat customers experience.

Front covers of English and Spanish brochures listing the services and resources of the Business Resource & Information EXchange (BRIX) at Newburgh Free Library

During the coming year, the program's value will be affirmed as staffing costs, materials acquisition and expenditures for services such as workshops and networking opportunies are incorporated into Newburgh Free Library's reference budget. The coordinator will explore additional partnership and funding possibilities to further assure the library's integral role in the business community. Our immigrant and minority entrepreneurs have too often experienced programs "full of sound and fury and signifying nothing." Through BRIX, we are committed to being a permanent resource for successful economic enterprise.

Works Cited

Linley, Rebecca and Bob Usherwood. *New Measures for the New Library: A Social Audit of Public Libraries;* http://panizzi.shef.ac.uk/cplis/social.htm

Lynch, Beverly P. "Public Library Service to Business." *Public Libraries* 37 (1998): 382–386.

Nerone, Fred. "SCORE Business Adviser: Averting small business failure." *Naples Daily News,* May 31, 1999; http://www.naplenews.com/today/business/d251710a.htm

"Newburgh Among Cities with Small Job-Growth Rate." *Times–Herald Record,* March 13, 1998: 57.

United States. Census Bureau. 1992 Economic Census. "Minority-Owned Business Enterprises"

United States. Small Business Administration. Office of Advocacy. Small Business Economic Indicators, 1998. "Executive Summary." March 2000; http://www.sba.gov/ADVO/stats/sbei98/pdf

SCHENECTADY

THE SCHAFFER LIBRARY
MULTICULTURAL WEB SITE PROJECTS

By Bruce Connolly and Gail M. Golderman

Union College, a private, liberal arts institution, with a strong commitment to diversity within a rapidly changing student and faculty population, defines its mission in terms of offering study experiences that "enable students to see the ways in which they are part of something larger — a community, a culture, and a world of many cultures." Programs in Latin American Studies, Africana Studies, and East Asian Studies demonstrate Union's commitment, as does its establishment of a Multicultural Resources Center, sponsorship of a conference on multicultural education, and the recent diversification of the reading list for the Freshman Preceptorial (FP) Program.

Schaffer Library's response to the college's commitment expresses itself through a variety of activities and projects — acquiring materials for new programs in Africana and East Asian Studies, conducting bibliographic instruction sessions for incoming Academic Opportunity Program students, and integrating bibliographic records of resources held by the Multicultural Resource Center and The Women's Studies Center into the library online catalog.

In late 1996, the authors produced a suite of Web-based multicultural guides, which incorporate most of what we have done within the library to serve Union's community. Schaffer Library's Web site, *Multicultural Resources*, with a link to *Multicultural Web Sites* and *Resources for Specific Groups* provides an integrated means of:

- identifying research materials – including print, AV, and electronic resources – available within the Schaffer Library collections
- providing instruction in the use of the online databases accessible through the library home page
- exploring remote Web sites exhibiting research value for academic work in multicultural studies.

Multicultural Web Sites consists of an annotated listing of specialized print reference sources, bibliographies, existing research guides, and sources of research materials including books from our own and other libraries and CD-ROM and online databases for locating journal articles. Section III is called *The Virtual Library: Relevant World-Wide Web Sites for Multicultural Research*, and we have attempted to be fairly selective by favoring research-oriented Web sites over those whose intent is more social, making sure that most of those selected are rich in unique content.

Resources for Specific Groups includes dedicated pages for:

General Multicultural Resources
African-American/Africana Studies
Asian American/East Asian Studies
Gay/Lesbian/Bisexual Research
India/Indian Studies
Latino-American/Latin American Research
Jewish American/Judaica Research
Middle Eastern Research
Native American Research
Women's Studies Research

Within each of the guides, we have made an effort to provide easy access to the Schaffer Library's Web catalog by identifying appropriate LC subject headings which are then hot-linked directly to library-owned multicultural books, journals, documents, and CDs. The *Multicultural Web Sites* page includes a link to Union's Multicultural Resource Center's Home Page, which gives social and cultural resources to complement the academic and research side.

We have also put the multicultural sites to work in the bibliographic instruction component of Union's Freshman Preceptorial Program. As part of the Skills Exercise that we have developed, students are asked to choose one of our multicultural sites dedicated to a specific group and then identify a specialized subject encyclopedia that they could use to gather basic information about their selected group. They then identify a source of data on this group, connect to one of the remote Web sites from among those we have incorporated into our page, and evaluate that site for its content, authority, organization, and design according to a set of criteria that we provide to them.

The *Skill Exercises* suggest that there are specialized references and statistical sources focused on a wide variety of people and subjects. It provides the experience of connecting to and evaluating remote information sources. And, finally, it advises students that they must make critical judgments about Internet resources before they can confidently incorporate the information they've found into a research project.

Diversity & Dialog Online

Since 1977, first-year students at Union have been required to participate in the FP Program, a writing-intensive, "great books" type of course. A cross-section of faculty from all departments teach in the preceptorial program, which means that all of them are teaching outside their areas of expertise to a greater or lesser extent. In 1994, the fundamental theme represented by the readings in the Freshman Preceptorial Program evolved from the more Western and traditional "Perception & Persuasion" into the more global "Dialog & Diversity." The revised preceptorial exposes the first-year student to a much less ethnocentric body of readings as it balances *Hamlet* with *The Mahabharata,* Plato with Lao Tzu, *The Bible* with *The Koran,* and Toni Morrison with Karl Marx.

Library involvement with the preceptorial program deepened in the summer of 1997 when Union College decided to pursue a grant from the Andrew W. Mellon Foundation for the purpose of introducing multimedia resources into the course. As part of the grant application process, we were asked to design sample Web pages that would not just illustrate what the college intended to accomplish with Mellon support but would also demonstrate Union's existing commitment to the overall endeavor.

We built *Dialog & Diversity: The Freshman Preceptorial Web Site* along the same basic lines as the individual documents within the existing "Web Research" series, which are intended for use within both the instructional and reference setting. The subtle, but fundamental, difference is that the preceptorial site aims to provide a context for students reading works from disciplines outside their majors, for faculty preceptors teaching a body of readings completely remote from their academic training, and for both students and preceptors examining material and ideas that come from entirely outside their cultural experience. The Web site intends to serve both students and preceptors by directing them to specific articles within the library's reference collection on the author, the author's times, and themes and concepts relevant to understanding a particular work.

Consistent with Mellon's intention of supporting efforts to incorporate multimedia resources into the preceptorial program, our site integrates links to articles from *Britannica Online* and other Web publications, to audio resources, and to electronic texts. A select group of academically relevant Web pages are given for each particular author and the context of the author's writings. Because dynamic links to appropriate books in the Schaffer Library online catalog are included along with direct links to research databases, each site can be used by preceptors as a convenient means of identifying research materials available within the library, of conducting demonstrations and searches of the various online databases, and of visiting remote Internet sites. *Dialog & Diversity* is a resource that aims to make the preceptorial readings more comprehensible by placing each work within its broader (social, historical, political, literary, philosophical and cultural) context. Because the library FP site integrates traditional library materials (reference books, monographs, CDs, videos) with online access to the library catalog, Internet resources, and subscription databases, it is a particularly useful vehicle for launching and guiding student research projects, as the following two examples illustrate:

1. The site for Olaudah Equiano, for example, directs students and faculty to:

    *   biographical articles from reference books such as *African American Writers* (Macmillan), *Black Literature Criticism* (Gale), *Encyclopedia of African-American Culture and History* (Macmillan)
    *   contextual background on the slave trade from *Encyclopedia of Africa South of the Sahara* and *The Historical and Cultural Atlas of African Americans*
    *   books on slavery in the Schaffer Library collection
    *   Web sites such as *The Equiano Foundation Online* at http://www.atomicage.com/equiano/, primary source materials, and our own *Multicultural Resources: African-American/Africana Studies* (http://www.union.edu/PUBLIC/LIBRARY/guide/mcafric.html)
    *   research databases "Historical Abstracts" and "Black Studies on Disc."

2. The site for *The Koran* offers:

- a biographical article on "Muhammad and the Religion of Islam" from *Britannica Online*
- contextual background on *The Koran* from *Encyclopedia of Islam* (Leiden), *The Encyclopedia of Religion* (Macmillan), *The Oxford Encyclopedia of the Modern Islamic World* (Oxford UP), and *Britannica Online*
- critical commentary from *Classical and Medieval Literature Criticism* (Gale)
- books in the Schaffer Library collection on Islam, Muhammad, and the history and social conditions of the Middle East
- Web sites such as *Ahlul Bayt Digital Islamic Library* at http://www.al-islam.org/organizations/dilp/ and *The Islam Page* at http://www.islamworld.net/
- online sources of audio recordings of Islamic prayers and readings from *The Koran*
- research databases such as "Historical Abstracts" and "Philosopher's Index"

Several factors combine to make working on the *Diversity & Dialog* site particularly satisfying. The first is that the site is playing an active and significant role in the education of both freshmen and the faculty who teach them. By carefully combing every relevant reference book and Internet resource, we have created a basic reading list for the self-education of faculty in the program. Likewise, for the student who wants to comprehend the circumstances from which a particular work emerged, we've delivered a vehicle for that pursuit. Furthermore, as a second-generation Web resource, the FP site incorporates and builds upon the work that went into our original suite of "Multicultural Resources" developed in 1996–97. In November of 1998 we presented our work on the site to a group of preceptors who immediately saw its potential as a valuable resource. Affirmation of our effort assumed a more concrete form when Union College was awarded one of the Mellon Foundation's grants.

Sites for Toni Morrison, Sor Juana Inés de la Cruz, Olaudah Equiano, *The Koran*, Plato, LaoTzu, Voltaire, Freud, Virginia Woolf, Henrik Ibsen, Shakespeare, Marx, Frederic Douglass, Sojourner Truth, Gabriel García Márquez, *The Bhagavad Gita*, and *The Mahabharata*, have been published so far.

Collection Building/Bridge Building

In the period since we first brought up the full complement of multicultural Web sites, their existence has begun to define new uses and new directions for us to pursue. Besides putting the Multicultural Guides to work as part of our library instruction efforts, we have seen that the energy devoted to the development of the multicultural sites has made us more conscious of gaps in our collection, and in turn, has provided the incentive to identify materials that we should be acquiring to fill those gaps. We have similarly discovered areas where we have had to begin doing our own reference tool building when existing print and Internet resources failed to provide the information we needed. We have also begun to get a sense of the less tangible rewards of our work.

Last year, one of our librarians initiated contact with members of Shakti, Union's South Asian student group, at a student activities fair and suggested that the group recommend a selection of Indian music CDs for the library to purchase. We were able to immediately provide them with three Indian music discographies—which form the basis of a CD collection development database being developed for Web publication—to help them make their choices. We also provided a list of Indian CDs already owned by the library. They were appreciative of the academic thoroughness of our Indian site, and impressed that we had asked for their input on what should be added to the library collection. They have since asked the librarian involved to serve as the group's faculty advisor.

Opportunities and Directions

Future projects involve plans for a "Terms Abroad Web Site" integrating basic reference sources, travel guides, news sources, country studies (online and in print), and relevant Web sites for students planning to visit another country. We are working on a discography of essential world music CDs for publication on the library home page, and we will continue our efforts to support diversity within the Freshman Preceptorial Program.

Online Access

Schaffer Library's *Multicultural Resources* Web site is published at:
http://www.union.edu/PUBLIC/LIBRARY/
guide/mcmenu.html
       The address for the Freshman Preceptorial site is:
http://www.union.edu/PUBLIC/LIBRARY/guide/FP-
menu.html, or choose the Web Research Guides and Freshman Preceptorial options on the Schaffer Library Home Page to visit them both:
http:// www.union.edu/PUBLIC/LIBRARY/index.html

       The Schaffer Library's Multicultural Web Site received NYLA's "Ethnic Services Round Table Multicultural Award" in 1997 and ALA's "GALE/EMIERT Multicultural Award" in 1999.

THE WORLD MUSIC PLAY LISTS

AN ONLINE COLLECTION-BUILDING RESOURCE
FOR LIBRARIANS AND LISTENERS

By Bruce Connolly

Starting with its premiere issue in the winter of 2000, *PLAY: The Online Music Reference Source for Librarians, Listeners, and Collection Builders,* began its existence as a Web-based resource compiled and edited by the author. *PLAY* is the tool I had been hunting for in order to help make my job as a library music collection builder easier and to satisfy my own curiosity as a listener. *PLAY* is a vehicle for identifying the year's best CDs and for determining which recordings should legitimately comprise a core collection for every genre. *PLAY* is my excuse for exploring music that I otherwise might have missed and my way of working through what it is that really makes a record outstanding. *PLAY* is how I motivate myself to keep abreast of what's happening in music in general and in music technology in particular. *PLAY* is also my set of bookmarks.

The *PLAY Lists* feature — a series of discographies representing the best CDs of the year and the decade, core collections in various musical genres, bibliographies of collection-building resources, and a running list of the year's best CD releases — are at the heart of *PLAY*. The *PLAY Lists* are essentially a research project which involves the collection of published sources of outstanding and recommended recordings, the development of a weighted rating scale that reflects the relative credibility of these sources, and the creation of a number of database files. The aim of this effort is to determine which CDs — by critical consensus — should be identified as the most outstanding recordings within a given genre.

PLAY deals with all musical genres, including, of course, popular world and folk music. The *PLAY List* feature showcases the best world music recordings for a given year, according to the reviewers and critics contributing to the music publications identified below. The ranking represents my attempt to determine whether a consensus emerges among world music authorities when some effort is made to quantify critical opinion. Nonetheless, these listings are not intended as the ultimate statement on artistic achievement but rather meant to serve as a roadmap for listeners who would like some direction when it comes to exploring new music. Additionally, the *PLAY Lists* are also meant to serve as a collection-building tool for librarians (and particularly for the non-specialist librarian)—who are frequently desperate for informed recommendations and have to prioritize their acquisitions decisions.

Among the *PLAY Lists* appearing in Vol. 1, No. 1 was "The Best World Music Recordings of 1999—A Critical Consensus." "First purchase" sets of Cuban, Afro-Pop, and Indian music CDs are planned along with more comprehensive core collection discographies for rap and reggae. *PLAY* also reviews world music CDs, magazines such as *Songlines* and *Irish Music*, and buying guides such as *MusicHound World* and *World Music: The Rough Guide*. The *Seeing Stars* feature tracks well-reviewed CDs in all genres.

The sources that I employ in building the World Music *PLAY Lists* include the following:

CD Buying Guides

All Music Guide: The Experts' Guide to the Best Blues Recordings. Edited by Michael Erlewine...[et al]. 3rd ed. San Francisco: Miller Freeman Books, 1997.

A Basic Music Library: Essential Scores and Sound Recordings. Compiled by the Music Library Association; Elizabeth

Davis, coordinating editor. Chicago: American Library Association, 1997.

The Encyclopedia of Popular Music. Compiled and edited by Colin Larkin. 3rd edition. London: MUZE UK Ltd., 1998.

The Garland Encyclopedia of World Music. Advisory editors, Bruno Nettl and Ruth M. Stone; founding editors, James Porter and Timothy Rice. New York: Garland Pub., 1998–

MusicHound World: The Essential Album Guide. Edited by Gary Graff, Josh Freedom du Lac and Jim McFarlin. Detroit: Visible Ink Press, 2000.

The Rolling Stone Album Guide. Edited by Anthony DeCurtis and James Henke with Holly George-Warren. New York: Random House, 1992.

World Music: The Rough Guide. Editors Simon Broughton ... [et al.]; contributing editor Kim Burton. London: Rough Guides Ltd., 1995.

World Music Magazines

The Beat
Folk Roots
Irish Music
Latin Beat

Music Magazines (General)

Down Beat
Jazziz
Mojo
Q

Rolling Stone
Spin

To visit the various *PLAY Lists,* connect to the PLAY Home Page at:
http:// www.union.edu/PUBLIC/LIBRARY/PLAY/index.html

PLAY: The Online Music Reference Source for Librarians, Listeners, and Collection Builders is compiled and edited solely by the author. The work has been supported via grants from the Union College Humanities Faculty Development Fund and the Schaffer Library Whitehorn Fund. It was recognized at the "Best Practices Awards Showcase" at the Online World 2000 Conference in San Diego.

SHIRLEY

¡BIENVENIDO A LA BIBLIOTECA!

LAUNCHING PUBLIC LIBRARY SERVICE TO
A SPANISH-SPEAKING COMMUNITY
ON SUBURBAN LONG ISLAND

By Laurie Hastings

"A Spanish-speaking staff member is now available to help you at the Mastics–Moriches–Shirley Community Library." These words, written on a bright yellow flyer, launched the library's first targeted service to our Spanish-speaking community. Starting in June 2000, the library began to offer assistance in Spanish on two nights per week. In September, we held our first National Hispanic Heritage Month celebration. After only six months, we are already noticing a dramatic increase in the number of Spanish-speaking patrons using the library. No new staff members were hired to implement this service. How the library began this groundbreaking initiative, including community analysis, planning, evaluation, and staffing issues, is the focus of this article. In other words, how a library with no Spanish-speaking professional staff, a neglected foreign language collection and no existing planned outreach to non-English speaking patrons launched a successful Spanish outreach program.

Situated on Long Island's South shore, the Mastics–Moriches–Shirley Community Library (MMSCL) is located approximately sixty miles east of New York City and serves the residents of the William Floyd School District. The total population served is approximately 55,000, and includes contractual service with the residents of South Manor and Eastport. The demographics for the library's service community have been evolving over the past few years. Specifically, there has been an unprecedented growth in the Hispanic population, and an intensive public relations analysis indicated that they were underserved by the Community Library, and were underrepresented as users. During an ongoing evaluation process that is described in this essay, it was decided that the MMSCL would launch a new service specifically focusing on the Spanish-speaking population. This project is described below.

Background

Established by the voters of the William Floyd School District in 1974, the MMSCL has historically served a predominantly blue-collar, working-class community with a large Italian and Irish population. The community is now experiencing a large influx of Spanish-speaking immigrants. The projected population statistics put out by the Long Island Regional Planning Board, along with the school district's enrollment statistics, indicates a Hispanic population of between 7 and 10 percent. (Hispanic school enrollment in the William Floyd School District in 1999–2000 was 11.56 percent.)

As the community was changing, the Community Library was experiencing some significant changes as well. After twenty-five years, the library's founding director retired and a new director was hired with the intent of carrying on our legacy of innovative and proactive library service. Looking to the future, our new director established seven focus groups within the library comprised of employees from all departments for the purpose of long-range planning and expediting select projects.

As the head of the "Marketing & PR" focus group, I was given the directive to lead a group in both promoting the library and its services, as well as targeting specific populations in the community who were underserved or unserved. Our group consists of two full-time Adult Services librarians, one full-time Children's Services librarian and the library's full-time Literacy Outreach Coordinator. We began in February 2000 and by May submitted the final draft of a mission statement and goals and objectives to the library's director.

The Mission Statement reads: "To increase community awareness of library resources, services and programs by developing and implementing an ongoing public relations plan." Our main goal is to make the Hispanic community more aware of library resources, services and programs, and to make these services accessible to Spanish-speaking community members. Our objectives for this goal include:

- implementing a bilingual service on a trial basis to assess its viability
- increasing staff awareness about the Hispanic population and educating them in the library's new initiative to serve this population
- increasing and organizing the Spanish language collection for adults and children including books, periodicals, music, movies, software, and electronic resources
- educating the Hispanic community regarding resources available through library technology
- translating select library publications into Spanish

"¿SABÍA USTED?"

"A Spanish-speaking staff member is now available to help you at the Mastics–Moriches–Shirley Community Library." We were able to avoid hiring additional staff for this new service by enlisting a library page, who is a Spanish-speaking college student, on Mondays and a native Spanish-speaking volunteer on Thursdays. The bilingual staff are situated at the Circulation Desk with a bright yellow sign that reads: "*¡Bienvenido! Estamos para ayudarles.*" (Greetings! We are here to help you.). They have been trained in the basic configuration and workings of the library, and serve as interpreters when necessary. We also set up a Spanish voice mailbox where patrons may leave a message in Spanish and receive a call back. Two thousand copies of the *¿Sabía usted?* (Did you know?) flyer describing these bilingual services were distributed around the community. With this first flyer, we committed to publicizing all relevant information in both Spanish and English. One thousand copies of *¿Sabía usted?* were sent to the local Catholic church. The remaining were distributed to other local churches, the local bodega, the school district's ESL department, supermarkets, banks, laundromats, etc. In addition, our local weekly newspaper graciously ran the advertisement for us several times in English and Spanish. It also appeared in the library's September newsletter.

The word began to spread and people began to come on Monday and Thursday evenings. What began as one or two became up to five or six contacts per night. The vast majority of questions have been about English instruction, computer instruction and library cards, along with requests for specific information or titles in Spanish.

The Translation Challenge

One of our biggest challenges has been getting material translated into Spanish. Since everything we write must be translated, we have learned that all written communication must be brief and to the point. Because none of the staff can write Spanish well, we had to quickly locate someone to provide us with written translations. We soon found a college student at SUNY Stony Brook who is majoring in languages and has studied Spanish translation. Paid on a per job basis, he began to translate for us, but we soon realized that translation into Spanish is not a simple matter. When we showed the translations to people from various countries, corrections were made based on the customs of the particular locale. Whoever read it next would make corrections again. Our heads began to spin, but we really wanted to start getting the word out, so we took the plunge with our September newsletter and included four articles in Spanish. Mistakes were made, some typographical and some grammatical, but we believe that everyone is receiving the message in the spirit that it is being delivered. "Keep it simple" has become our mantra!

Developing and Organizing the Collection

The library had a very small Spanish language collection for adults and it was tucked away in a corner and sorely neglected. Materials in Spanish for children were interfiled with English material. Both public service departments decided to create separate Spanish language collections and promote them actively. The Adult Department began subscriptions to eight new Spanish magazines and a newspaper. These are now prominently displayed in the center of the library, along with Spanish books, CD-ROMs, bibliographies, discographies, pamphlets and flyers. A wealth of multicultural resources has been added to the library's databases and Web site. There has also been a big effort to obtain a rich variety of Latin and Spanish music on compact disk. Finally, we separated our existing Spanish language movie collection, and enriched it with popular films either dubbed or subtitled in Spanish. The Children's Department has separated its Spanish language collection and displays it prominently in the children's room. All these displays must be refreshed on a daily basis as the materials are racing off the shelves!

Celebrating National Hispanic Heritage Month

With our Spanish service framework in place, we decided that the library would create its first significant celebration of National Hispanic Heritage Month, September 15–October 15. One of the high points of our celebration was a *Family Fiesta* held on Saturday, September 23 from 6:30–9:30 P.M. The purpose of the *Fiesta* was to invite the Spanish-speaking community into the library to learn about the wonderful materials and services that we offer. We wanted to do this in a manner that welcomed the whole family at once. We arranged to have many people present at the *Fiesta* who were able to translate, including students and their teacher from the high school's Spanish Club. With approximately fifty people attending, from toddlers to seniors, the *Family Fiesta* was held in our large meeting hall that was decorated with balloons, posters and festive tablecloths, and refreshments were provided. A large variety of Spanish language materials for adults and children were displayed, and six computers for adults and children with Internet and CD-ROM access were set up. A staff member taught handicrafts to the children and there was a drawing table. Raffles and a screening of the family movie, *Stuart Little*, in Spanish, wrapped up the evening's festivities. The *Fiesta* was a wonderful opportunity for the staff and the community to come together, share information and get to know each other better. It was a resounding success!

The Mastics–Moriches–Shirley Community Library used the cover of its September 2000 newsletter to advertise its first celebration of Hispanic Heritage Month

In addition to the *Fiesta*, the library has celebrated Hispanic Heritage Month with a prominent display of large posters of famous Hispanics and attractive table displays with materials in

Spanish and in English about Hispanics. There were children's craft programs on a Hispanic theme, and movies in Spanish for adults and children. Finally, on October 7th, the library's Friends of the Arts organization presented a performance by the world class ensemble, *Amigos de la Zarzuela*, featuring outstanding artists from Cuba, Puerto Rico, and Spain performing music and dance of the zarzuela, which is the traditional musical theatre of Spain.

Future Challenges and Directions

Since this was the library's first effort to target the Spanish-speaking community, it did not take place without reaction from the community and the staff. Although most of the staff were supportive, there were some that expressed their unhappiness or resentment. "Why are you only doing this for the Hispanic community? What about the Italians (the Asians, the Turks, etc.)?" Some of the reactions from the public included, "Is the library turning Spanish?" and, "They will never learn how to speak English if you give them material in Spanish!" Our focus group is aware of these concerns, and is working toward increasing understanding and empathy among the staff and public.

The Community Library's administration and Board of Trustees is committed to this effort to serve this segment of the population who have not taken advantage of their library. Even after such a short time, we are already seeing a change in our usage. Ever increasing numbers of Spanish-speaking patrons are coming in and approaching the staff. The request for English language instruction has soared, and we are currently training thirty new volunteer tutors through our Literacy Volunteers office. We are also planning on presenting computer instruction in Spanish as soon as we are able. Finally, it is our hope that after the six-month trial of providing assistance in Spanish, the library will commit to hiring Spanish-speaking employees in order to continue this very important and exciting new service.

UTICA

THE UTICA PUBLIC LIBRARY AND THE MOHAWK VALLEY RESOURCE CENTER FOR REFUGEES

BY DARBY O'BRIEN

The city of Utica is nestled in the center of New York State. On the banks of the Mohawk River and the Barge Canal, adjacent to the New York State Thruway, the ribbon of highway that connects all the major cities in the state, it is the gateway to the Adirondacks and one-time hub for rail service in upstate New York. When my grandmother's family summered in the Adirondacks prior to World War II, they changed trains in Utica. In those days Utica was a town of mills and factories and drew many immigrants: Welsh, Irish, Polish, Lebanese, Italian, African American and German. Thus, Utica has long been a city rich in diverse ethnic heritage. The last quarter of the twentieth century has brought a new wave of immigrants to the Utica area. These newcomers are refugees and they come from many places throughout the world including Vietnam, Bosnia, the Former Soviet Union and Burma, to name a few. They come with little more than the clothes on their backs and have often traveled a harrowing journey before arriving in Utica. These refugees have come to Utica because of the Mohawk Valley Resource Center for Refugees, which is sponsored by the Lutheran Immigration and Refugee Service. The Center has the responsibility of resettling the refugees and helping them find employment within six months of their arrival. The forty-seven employees (forty-two are former refugees) provide interpreter services for clients in their interactions with social service agencies, the educational system, medical services, and potential employers. Since 1991, over 6,000 refugees have been helped through the

Center and 80 percent of those have remained in the area permanently with nearly all settling in Utica. The Center also provides on-going services for the refugees through English as a Second Language classes and citizenship counseling.

The Utica Public Library and the Mohawk Valley Resource Center for Refugees are neighbors. Both are located on the city's main street. They are also located adjacent to the older neighborhoods in the city where many of the refugees initially live. Because of the library's proximity to the Center and their homes, many of the refugees use the library from the day they arrive in Utica.

Over the years formal and informal programs have been initiated between the Center and the library. In the early 1990s, as the number of refugees increased, the immediate need was to expand the foreign language collection to include materials in Russian, Serbo-Croatian and Vietnamese. Central Book Aid (state monies given to a designated central library) has been used to purchase adult books. The New York Newspaper Foundation awarded the library a $5,000 grant to purchase children's books in these languages. The Center recently received a grant to purchase books for the library. The library has also paid the mailing costs to have books sent from Bosnia to Utica. We have relied on Center staff and clients to assist with the book selection process.

During the refugees' initial involvement with the Center, they receive a tour of the library and are encouraged to receive library cards. Many of them become enthusiastic library users and there are two areas that grab their attention. The first is the video collection. They are daily video borrowers, and viewing the videos helps them to improve their English skills. The second is the library's access to the Internet. The refugees are able to maintain contact through e-mail with their friends and relatives who have either remained in their homelands or have immigrated to different places on the globe. Also they are able to keep abreast of news in their homelands through Web sites written in their own languages.

The children, especially, participate in the regular library programs. This past spring the library sponsored an Image Writing Lab. During the course of this three-month program each child created and produced his/her own illustrated book. Vietnamese, Bosnian and Russian children completed the project. The library received a Parent and Child Library Services grant and a Rotary International grant, which supported the position of a tutor who helped the children with their homework and using the computers. Currently approximately 25 percent of the children using the library come from refugee families.

Newcomers to the United States have long found a welcome haven in the local public library. The Utica Public Library has continued this tradition through its partnerships with the Mohawk Valley Resource Center for Refugees. The future will find this connection expanding and strengthening.

CONTRIBUTORS

Kristine Alpi, Information Services Librarian, Samuel J. Wood Library, Weill Medical College of Cornell University, New York City; kalpi@att.net

Zahra M. Baird, Children's Librarian, Scarsdale Public Library (Westchester Library System); zbaird@westchesterlibraries.org

Claudia Blackler, Director, Greenwich Free Library; blackler@capital.net

Mary F. Bobinski, Director, Amherst Public Library; bobinskim@buffalolib.org

Thomas W. Brogan, Branch Manager, Bushwick Branch, Brooklyn Public Library; t.brogan@brooklynpubliclibrary.org

Dorothy Buice, Librarian, Science and Industry Division, Central Library, Brooklyn Public Library (former Assistant Branch Librarian, Sunset Park Branch, Brooklyn Public Library); d.buice@brooklynpubliclibrary.org

Cara Jane Burton, Director, Solvay Public Library (former Director of LaFayette Public Library); caraburt@ocpl.lib.ny.us

Brigid A. Cahalan, Bronx Community Outreach Specialist, The New York Public Library; bcahalan@nypl.org

David Callahan, Senior Film/Video Librarian, Donnell Library Media Center, The New York Public Library; dcallahan@nypl.org

Ronald S. Chan, Supervising Branch Librarian, Chatham Square Regional Branch, The New York Public Library; rchan@nypl.org

Wai Sze Chan, Information & Data Analysis Librarian, New Americans Program, Queens Borough Public Library; wchan@queenslibrary.org

David Cohen, Director, EMIE, Queens College (City University of New York); davidc@qc1.qc.edu

Bruce Connolly, Reference Librarian, Schaffer Library, Union College, Schenectady; connollb@union.edu

Esther Dean, Director, Amsterdam Public Library; amslib@telenet.net

Jane Fisher, Coordinator, Office of Information Services, The New York Public Library; jfisher@nypl.org

Madelyn Folino, Director, Florida (N.Y.) Public Library; mfolino@rcls.org

Patricia Gallagher, Special Projects Coordinator, The New York Academy of Medicine Library; pgallagher@nyam.org

Fred J. Gitner, Assistant Head, New Americans Program, Queens Borough Public Library; fgitner@queenslibrary.org

Gail M. Golderman, Electronic Media Librarian, Schaffer Library, Union College, Schenectady; goldermg@union.edu

Harriet Gottfried, Assistant Coordinator, Office of Community Outreach Services, The New York Public Library; hgottfried@nypl.org

Laurie Hastings, Assistant Director and Head of Reference & Adult Services, Mastics–Moriches–Shirley Community Library, Shirley; lhasting@suffolk.lib.ny.us

Dorothy Holt, Reference/Youth Services Librarian, Guilderland Public Library; dotcomlil@aol.com

Suzanne Jacobs, Librarian II, Department of Extension Services, Urban Services Division, Buffalo & Erie County Public Library; jacobss@buffalolib.org

Glendora Johnson-Cooper, Associate Librarian/Collection Development Coordinator, Oscar A. Silverman Undergraduate Library, and Program Manager, Library Internship/Residency Program, University at Buffalo; gjcooper@acsu.buffalo.edu

Irina A. Kuharets, Senior Librarian/Slavic Specialist, Donnell World Languages Collection, The New York Public Library; ikuharets@nypl.org

Stephan Likosky, Correctional Services Librarian, Office of Community Outreach Services, The New York Public Library; slikosky@nypl.org

Anne McCarthy Kennedy, Business Resource Coordinator, Newburgh Free Library; kenna@rcls.org

Christine McDonald, Director, Crandall Public Library, Glens Falls; mcdonald@crandalllibrary.org

Darby O'Brien, Director, Utica Public Library; obrien@midyork.lib.ny.us

Robin Osborne, Adult and Outreach Services Consultant, Westchester Library System, Ardsley; rosborne@wlsmail.org

Jennifer L. Ransom, Reference Librarian, Mother Irene Gill Library, The College of New Rochelle; jransom@cnr.edu

Stanley A. Ransom, former Director of the Huntington (L.I.) Public Library and former Director of the Clinton–Essex–Franklin Library System, Plattsburgh; sransom@northnet.org

Sally Romano, Children's Librarian, Amsterdam Public Library; amslib@telenet.net

Caren Shilling Koh, Children's Materials Specialist, Programs and Services Department, Queens Borough Public Library; cshilling@queenslibrary.org

Bosiljka Stevanovic, Principal Librarian, World Languages Collection, Donnell Library Center, The New York Public Library; bstevanovic@nypl.org

Patricia Stocker, Assistant Director, Pioneer Library System, Canandaigua; pstocker@pls-net.org

SUBJECT INDEX

Note: Page number refers to the first page of the article where the material pertaining to the subject can be found